RESTART

YOUR CHURCH

DOTTIE ESCOBEDO-FRANK

Abingdon Press
Nashville

ReStart Your Church

Library of Congress Cataloging-in-Publication Data

Escobedo-Frank, Dottie.
  reStart your church / Dottie Escobedo-Frank.
    pages cm
  Includes bibliographical references.
  ISBN 978-1-4267-4339-9 (Book - Paperback / Trade Paperback) 1. Church renewal—United States.
I. Title.
  BR526.E83 2012
  262.001'7—dc23

                                                                                          2012034283

12 13 14 15 16 17 18 19 20 21—10 9 8 7 6 5 4 3 2 1

MANUFACTURED IN THE UNITED STATES OF AMERICA

CONTENTS

BEGINNING THOUGHTS

I don't want to write a "how-to" book. I've never wanted to provide a list of action items for someone to follow a certain way in order to achieve the promise of a certain outcome. That thought makes my stomach turn.

Instead, I recognize that I am part of a larger conversation about what is going on with our churches, and it is my hope that this book is a voice in the global conversation. As I write this, I am finishing up my time with the Western Jurisdiction's Clergywomen's Consultation in Reno. We spent some of our time talking about the upcoming General Conference of 2012, and how that decision-making body might affect our future in The United Methodist Church. I am aware, as we share our ideas about the changes needed in the greater church, that the quickest way to make these changes occur in our structure is to make radical shifts in our congregations. No policy, polity, or planning team can do what the local congregation, called by God and with their hearts set on God, can do. I am especially aware that some of the quickest and deepest changes are likely to happen in the smallest of congregations.

So I write this as a manual of hope. Not a document on how to get there, but rather a reminder of the journey we have always been on, and of the God who has always been about miracles in our midst. I pray you rise up and transform yourselves, your families, and your churches. For in doing this, the greater church will follow.

And, as an author, I have one more postscript of acknowledgment. We live in a world where we receive so much information every day that we can't differentiate an original thought from what we heard from someone else. Perhaps most of our musings and ramblings are a compilation of ideas that come from others in our lives. The idea that an author can write a few pages without committing the sin of stealing from another author is impossible today. We can provide quotation marks as a way to give recognition for direct verbiage, but who can quote the compilation of ideas that creates a seemingly new idea when, in reality, it has already been said or thought?

What we see happening is that the collective conscious is deeply rooted in our lives. Our technological communication tools import a global consciousness deep into our being. In Ecclesiastes 1:9, this recognition of "collective conscious" is stated in this way: "There's nothing new under the sun."

This ancient axiom is magnified today by Internet news, smart phones, Pandora radio, GPS, text messaging, Skype, and on and on. It is harder today to turn off the collective conscious voice than at any other time in our history. We walk around with our work connected to our phones, which never leave our possession. Our little machines notify us every time someone sends us an e-mail, Facebook message, tweet, or even an old-fashioned telephone call. The collective conscious is on nearly 24-7.

And so I shudder at the possibility of describing someone else's ideas as if they are my own. It is very possible that nothing in this book was my thought first, but that it all belongs to the connected world we live in. So I apologize up front, and yet I don't. For I know I live in a world where the free flow of ideas changes the notion of copying. If your idea is here, remember another axiom uttered long ago by Charles Caleb Colton: "Imitation is the sincerest form of flattery."

LOOKING FOR A RESTART

reStart

The haunting sounds and lyrics of Colbie Caillat's song "Bubbly" make me think of a life waking out of a deep sleep . . .

> I've been asleep for a while now
> You tucked me in just like a child now.

The song is playful, speaking of waking and sleeping. But what haunts me in this song is the phrase "I've been asleep for a while now." I resonate with the words as I think about many of our churches. We've been asleep. We've even been called "the sleeping giant."[1] We are so asleep that one of the phrases used to bring calm to pastors and church leaders is "Just lay low." Another is "Fly under the radar." The message of these phrases is to not make too much noise, do anything that gets noticed, or ruffle any feathers. The "wisdom" is to hang tight and hope that in time things will change. Contrast this with the words of the founder of the Methodist movement, John Wesley: "I set myself on fire and they come to see me burn."[2]

Instead of burning with Wesley's passion, we are in such a profound state of sleep that we take comfort in sleeping more. But it can't last forever. Eventually we are forced to wake up. Since our period of slumber has been so long and so deep, we are just beginning to wake up and take notice of a few things:

1. We see that the world has changed and the church hasn't kept up.

2. We see that many churches are closing, and the empty seats are alarming.

3. We see that we are growing old, even to the precipice of death.

4. We notice that young people are mostly absent, or are present but with a sense of disgust.

5. We are not keeping up fiscally, numerically, or, most importantly, spiritually.

6. We have become the dead, lifeless body that our original Reformers warned us about.[3]

7. We understand that we are not really making or becoming disciples of Jesus Christ.

If you are in a church that is in this state, and according to Thom Rainer, 94 percent of American churches are in this decline,[4] then perhaps we can face this together.

I have some experience in dying churches. Having served in four churches, three of which were in dire straits, I know the path from decline and death to life. It is well-worn for me, as it perhaps is for you. The problem is that many of us get so discouraged along the way that instead of pursuing the dream of life, we remain in a place of comfortable boredom, napping away our time in the setting we call "church." Our passion gets beaten out of us. Our voices get quieted. Our courage wanes. It is the natural consequence of ministry in an environment of decline.

In the best-case scenario, the place we find ourselves in is what author and entrepreneur Seth Godin describes as "the Dip." "The Dip is the long slog between starting and mastery."[5] It is that part of work where things get hard, and not so fun, and the payoff seems nonexistent. Godin states that most people quit in the Dip whereas a few make it through and come out as masters of their arena. Some Dips need to be avoided at all costs, because they will become *Cul-de-Sacs*, French for "dead ends."[6] Dead ends go nowhere. They are a waste of time and resources. They are places where energy gets trapped and becomes stale. Many of us find ourselves in dead ends. If this is our current place, he states, we must quit. In the dead end, we must quit.

What we have to recognize is the difference between the Dip and the Cul-de-Sac. One leads to a beneficial end. The other remains in the same spot. Have you found yourself in a Cul-de-Sac church, or are you going through the long, arduous process of the Dip? It is important to find out which is true in your situation. The outcome is a life-and-death concern.

ReStart is about churches that have been in the Cul-de-Sac for decades. For them, hope is found when we figure out what must be learned, set aside the old ways, and begin again. To begin again is not just to hit the refresh button on your computer. It is more like when your computer has frozen and the only way out, short of going to the computer store or a technician, is to turn everything off, wait a few minutes, and restart it. When this happens, the previous problems become unimportant (in most cases) and the start is fresh, as if the problem and the past were not even there.

ReStart is about choosing new life for your church. Restarting is having the courage to sell everything and create a new life. Restarting acknowledges that a previous way existed, but it does not rely on that information to choose the path of today.

To restart your church means to embrace the grief that will surely be yours. It means to acknowledge death, seek resurrection, and walk forward on an unknown path.

Restarting means being the church that Jesus meant us to be. At some point in its history, every church is called to restart. Truly, the choice is to restart or die. Either/or. Not a continuum. Not a process. Not easy.

Since the very beginning, as a pastor learning to serve in near-dead churches, I have wanted to write a letter to the congregation. But I have never had the courage. Instead, I have led step-by-step, learning, following, and sometimes bulldozing ahead, leaving sure destruction in the wake of my cowardice. But what I have really wanted to do was have a frank and honest discussion about the church with a group of people who could put aside their traditions and their pain in order to forge a new way to go forward. This book is my attempt at that letter. If I could, I would read it out loud in front of your church. But I can't, and so, instead, I write this in the public arena, begging my current church to hear and risk the future that Christ intended for us. And I ask for every church community that studies these pages to be brutally honest with themselves and forgiving of the pain. It does us no good to lie to ourselves. Truth is the great liberator. When we set ourselves free from the untruth, we are ready to see Jesus in new ways.

I believe that Jesus would have us do no other.

The Reason for a ReStart

According to one report, 188,000 orthodox churches in America today are in need of a restart. The United States has 200,000 orthodox Christian churches, and 300,000 churches overall.[7] What recent history has made very clear is that the mainline church in America is dying. Thom Rainer, in a U.S. study of 1,159 churches (2002), said that 94 percent of American churches are in decline.[8] Recent church attendance records show that in America, real attendance numbers are not near 40 percent as previously reported, but a shocking 17.7 percent (2004). These numbers also report a trend for growth in the smallest (attendance of less than 49) and the largest (attendance of more than 2,000) churches, while reporting a sharp decline in medium-sized churches.[9] Note the statistics, for example, of two mainline denominations from the Association of Religion Data Archives (ARDA):

The United Methodist Church			
1968	41,901 churches	10,990,720 members	33,236 clergy
2005	34,397 churches	7,995,456 members	45,158 clergy

Evangelical Lutheran Church in America			
1987	11,133 churches	5,288,230 members	17,052 clergy
2006	10,470 churches	4,774,203 members	17,655 clergy

The data from ARDA[10] shows that not only did 7,504 United Methodist churches die between 1968 and 2005 but also membership declined by just under three million in the same period. During this time, the number of clergy, caring for fewer churches, increased by 11,922! The statistics for the Evangelical Lutheran Church in America are similar (these statistics cover a shorter period of time, between 1987 and 2006). A total of 663 churches have died, membership has dropped by 514,027, and the number of clergy has increased by 603. We are spending more money on clergy for fewer churches and fewer members. Something is wrong with this picture. These statistics bear out the "writing on the wall" of the state of crisis in the mainline church.

Some churches are still alive but declining rapidly. Some are near death, clinging to what once was as the hope for the future. As a result of the obvious near-death experiences of congregations, denominational structures are looking for ways to "revitalize" churches. Revitalization means taking what is and making it alive again. It tends to use current leadership, current understandings of what it means to be a church, current locations, and current worship styles. Revitalization makes an assumption that what is was once vital and, therefore, can be vital again, if we do the same, only better. So churches increase programs, dollars spent, and formulas adopted in order to bring the *re–* into revitalization. The prefix *re–* means "back to the original place."[11] Revitalization implies stepping back in time to recapture a period when the church's role in society was vital. A church seeking revitalization typically does more of the same, but in a hyped-up fashion.

Decades of honest labor and reams of pages written about this process, however, have shown us that revitalization is, on the whole, not working. It is, at best, bringing about slow, incremental change over a long period of time. In the medium, it is wearing out pastors and church leaders so that pastors end up leaving pulpits and laity end up leaving churches.[12] At worst, revitalization is either turning churches into places of hospice care or prolonging the agonizing death of a community of faith.

There must be a new way. Or there must be many new ways. I am making a new proposition—or perhaps it is an old one. Since the central story of our faith is the story of death and resurrection, churches need to find ways to live out this story. We all want to live the resurrection part of our faith, but we are unwilling to witness death in our midst so that resurrection can also be seen. We fight our own story, claiming, despite decades of evidence to the contrary, that revitalization of the church is possible.

We must make a drastic move away from revitalization and into the death and resurrection of the church. We must remember the words of the Scriptures, which say,

> Look, fool! When you put a seed into the ground, it doesn't come back to life unless it dies. What you put in the ground doesn't have the shape that it will have, but it's a bare grain of wheat or some other seed. God gives it the sort of shape that he chooses, and he gives each of the seeds its own shape. (1 Corinthians 15:36-38)

We persist in trying to shape our lives and resist the reshaping that comes in the form of our death-and-resurrection moments. We so desperately want to control life that we forget God is the one who brings new life. And when God brings new life, God brings a new shape. Our future is in God's hands, not ours. We try to control others when we ourselves feel out of control. Our churches are crashing, and we don't know what to do about it. We feel helpless, maybe hopeless. And our reaction is to control more. But God's way is to release our need to be in charge and give it over to God. We might as well go God's way, since our way hasn't been working for quite some time.

Your reStart

Your church may be in desperate need of a restart. Being willing to start over requires being comfortable with disorder.

Thomas Bandy writes of the need for religious leaders to move away from hierarchical communication and management of a vision. Instead, Bandy calls for giving in to the chaos that occurs during times of transformation. Too many church pastors are managers who spend all their time attending meetings, focusing on details, and controlling outcomes. I know because I have been there. But what is needed are leaders who will attend to the vision and attend to the Holy Spirit, seeking only to follow God's lead.[13] Bandy describes these new leaders in this way:

> Their commitment to *moderation* reflects their celebration of holistic health, their resistance to work addictions, and their appreciation for personal growth.
>
> Their commitment to *cooperation* reflects their readiness to "let go" of control, honor parallel leadership, and empower team.
>
> Their commitment to *poverty* reflects their priority for relational over material values, renunciation of economic entitlements, and compassion for the oppressed.
>
> Their commitment to *chastity* reflects their single-minded pursuit of God's mission, the simplicity of their lifestyle, and the sincerity of their ministry.
>
> Their commitment to *fidelity* reflects their loyalty to their personal, covenanted relationships to spouse and family.[14]

The shift from primary allegiance to the institutional church to loyalty to loving God, loving neighbor, and loving self is one that is transforming the face of the church. Transformational pastors are not interested in the structures that have failed the church but are focused on finding God's way for being the church today. They are willing to change, and to live into the intuitive knowledge that healthy pastors create healthy environments. These issues are the places where death is occurring and where God's resurrection possibilities exist.

Recognizing the Nearness of Death

When I was a social worker, I worked in the pediatric intensive-care unit of a local hospital. I was part of a team that responded to emergency room calls as new patients were being transported in following traumatic events. Often these children were close to death, and it was my job to find the parents and help them through the difficult moments of uncertainty. Moments when you don't know whether your child is going to live or die are extremely heart-wrenching, as you can imagine. Sometimes we stood in the room by a child as his or her heart stopped. The doctors and nurses would furiously work to save the child's life, as one, like a ballet dance team that knew how to work together to make something beautiful happen.

I have watched a child flatline while the mother and I held our breaths and our hands in prayer. Sometimes it was my job to pick the mama or daddy up off the floor as their baby died in front of our eyes. And sometimes it was our joy to see that child go from the pause of death to the breath of life. When that happened, the tears flowed freely, and the alleluias burst out of shut-down mouths. But I know now that both death and life silenced me, humbled me, and opened me to a pain and joy that I had not imagined.

Death is hard. Resurrection is a miracle. The death-and-resurrection cycle is our life.

The June 2010 issue of *Knowledge* magazine contains an article titled "The Real Flatliners," which tells the story of a surgeon, John

Elefteriades, who suspends his patients in death for twenty minutes or more in order to perform an operation. The patient lies on the table with the supportive heart-lung machine performing breath and circulation cycles. The person's body temperature has been cooled to about 66 degrees Fahrenheit. The doctor calls for the machine to stop. The patient is dead. No blood is flowing. No circulation or breath cycle. Everything, including the heart, lungs, and brain, ceases to function. This procedure is called Deep Hypothermic Circulatory Arrest, and the patient is clinically in a state of death. At this point the doctor performs surgery on the heart. During surgery someone regularly calls out the time so they can keep track of how long the patient has been dead. When he is finished, the doctor asks for a small amount of blood to begin to be circulated in the body, then the heart-lung machine assists, and the body is gradually warmed. And the patient comes back to life.[15]

Dr. Elefteriades speaks of deep hypothermia in this way:

> If medicine could extend the period people can stay in deep hypothermia while protecting that "wiring," the applications would be astounding—from buying time for patients awaiting organ donation to preventing fatal blood loss on the battlefield.[16]

Colleen Shaddox, the reporter and writer of "The Real Flatliners," calls it this way: "Death can be good for you."[17]

Some of our churches have been in "Deep Hypothermic Circulatory Arrest," and what we don't recognize is that this could be a good sign. For out of death . . . comes life!

The first church I served, Liberty United Methodist Church, was a small rural church that had a new pastor every year or two. They called themselves the "learning church," the place where pastors learned how to be a pastor. They taught me much, and they shaped me for ministry in the future. This committed community held the church together despite the continual flow of pastoral visitorship.

The next church, Mission Bell United Methodist Church, was near death when I arrived. They were on the emergency room table, wondering if they would live or die. I wondered too. This community looked death full in the face and cried out to God for life. And God breathed life into the small community through landscaping, planting a garden of beauty, and bringing children to the church community. God performed a miracle on the operating table. Many things died there before God breathed life into Mission Bell.

At the next church I served, I was mostly a witness of change. During my two years there I watched Community Church of Joy, a Lutheran megachurch, begin to go through a process of changing direction. In my short witness to this community, death, pain, and agonizing struggle were the rule of the day as the huge ship was turning around. It has endured the transition, and is moving forward, but that story belongs to someone else, since I was merely a privileged witness to the process of change.

I now serve at CrossRoads United Methodist Church in Phoenix, Arizona. When I came, we were a church of about sixty to one hundred people in worship, Anglo, with an average age in the eighties. Now we are double that in worship, much younger, and much more diverse, due to adding a second worship service. And we are reaching out to our community in service, including a group of homeless folk and approximately one hundred Hispanic children and their families. These do not normally attend our worship, but they are part of the outreach of our love.

We are not "there" yet. We still have major deaths ahead of us. Our church has suffered a year and a half of hell, where we didn't really look like the church on the inside, even as we did the work of the church on the outside. We are now at a place where we feel pain so deeply that we know it is time to let go and allow God to find the way for us. We are no longer trying to create the path forward. We are willing to die some, and we are willing to die a lot, and we are willing to die all the way, so that God can live in our midst. Don't get me wrong. It is not fun. But it is God's way, and when we trust in our God, the breath of the Holy Spirit comes back, and we learn to live differently, changed, and we become born again.

The church needs to learn from those who face death daily. *Death is good for us.* I don't say it is desired or that we understand it. I just know we must allow for the God of life and death to be God. When we allow for death, we find the life we seek. We need to trust that God will bring to life what God wants to bring to life. We need to stop trying to control, or stop, death so that God can move in our churches and in our living and in our dying.

It is time to live out our central story.

Are you ready to wake up in order to die some? That is the only way out. The only way to go through grief is to go *through* it. There is no healthy shortcut. There is no miracle program. There is no easy answer. Every step forward is closer to the new thing, but it is also closer to the crux of pain. The crux of pain is the same thing as the cross of Christ. We are people of the cross, and yet we act like Easter requires no cross. But it does. It requires nothing old except the cross. The old can be remembered with fondness, but it cannot be essential in the new thing that God is up to.

A decision to start over is a choice of dying, of waking up, and of being in love again. I do not recommend this journey unless you truly understand the pain of grief. Until then, it is pointless to go forward, pretending you want to change. This shift requires desire, courage, and endurance. If you are not ready, put this book down and walk away. Maybe this isn't your time.

But if you are desperate for God to show up in your heart and in your church, then I encourage you to keep on going through. If you are tired of sleeping away while the faith of your children and grand-children withers away, then I call out an invitation to come on this journey. If you are disgusted with your almost-love and almost-lovers, then I invite you to Real Love.

My three-year-old grandson, Niko, was a lover of his pacifier. He used it for comfort, he went to sleep with it, he ate with it, and he talked with it. If you tried to take it out of his mouth, he would bite down on it and hold it fast in his mouth. He had this habit of taking it out of his mouth, putting food into his mouth, and then sticking it quickly back in his mouth as he chewed. Sometimes when he went to eat, he forgot that his pacifier was not in his mouth, and his hand would reach out to take out what was not in his mouth. So engrained was his habit that the rest of his body was attuned to his pacifier. He called it his "fafier," but mostly it sounded like he was calling it his "fire."

One day his parents talked to him about giving up his pacifier. They told him he could trade it in for a toy of his choice. So they made a trip to the toy store, and Niko picked out a helicopter as his toy of choice. Niko also loved helicopters. He called them "hocca-planes," which is his version of helicopter-plane. He always paired those two things because, well, they both flew in the sky. So he found a beautiful "hocca-plane," and handed the cashier his "fire" as a trade. He went home and was remarkably okay for someone who had been so hooked on a pacifier.

We noticed some new things in Niko as he gave up his pacifier. His language improved greatly. Suddenly we all understood what he was trying to say, and we were amazed at the clarity of his voice and the depth of his thinking. He engaged his world differently, making his point known and inserting himself into conversations more. He looked more like a young boy and less like a large baby.

But one day, Niko had a meltdown, and his mom, Sara, found him sucking on his baby sister's pacifier behind the chair. She explained that he was big now and didn't need the pacifier and had traded it in for his helicopter. He responded immediately that he wanted to "throw his hocca-plane in the trash and get his fire back!" The old and familiar is such a difficult habit to break. Niko wanted to throw away the new thing and get his old thing back.

I love the phrase he used: "I want my fire back!" Sometimes we think we can do away with the new thing that is happening and at the same time, get our fire back. But it doesn't work that way. The new thing requires letting go of the old thing. And Niko perhaps prophesied what we all want. We want our fire back.

It is possible to start over. Our God is in the start-over business. Lean in, let go, and listen. God is calling us to something that could be like heaven on earth. I, for one, am begging to change, begging to be a real church.[18] I am hoping for a restart, and I don't know much about it, but I will think out loud so we can learn together. I know I can't do this alone. We need one another to whisper words of courage as we begin again. Come along and love your way forward. It won't be no ways easy.

The world is hungry for God while the church is grieving over the past. But in the Methodist tradition, there was always fire: fire for God, fire for God's people, and fire for heaven on earth.

Niko went up to bed and got his needed rest. He didn't seek that particular past again. But he was on to something familiar. Like Niko, I want the fire back.

THE SEMIOTICS OF DEATH

reSurrection

You've Gotta Die a Little. . . .
Well, You've Gotta Die a Lot

John Martyn wrote the lyrics to a song sung by Dean Martin called "The Glory of Love." The words are significant for the church:

> You've got to laugh a little, cry a little
> Sometimes let your poor heart die a
> little.

Love comes with a price. It cost Jesus something very great to love you and to form the church. It cost him his life. Jesus died because of a great love. He didn't die because of a feeling, or a romantic idea, or a little friendship. Jesus' love was so great that he was willing to die a terrible death so that we could be loved.

15

While we struggle with the logic of Jesus' death and resurrection, this is still the central story of our church. It's a beautiful, tragic, hopeful story that centers us as a people called Christians. But one of our problems is that we have become so enamored with the end of the story that we forget the heart of the story. Jesus rose from *death*. And so we remember, painfully, that resurrection requires some dying.

What needs to die in your church? One way to figure out what needs to die is to ask yourself, *If Jesus came into this church, which tables would he turn over in anger?* What would Jesus look at, raise up, and overthrow for the sake of the kingdom of God? Often the things we are working on have nothing to do with kingdom living or "kindom" loving. So where could you imagine Jesus with righteous anger in your setting? This is an important question because it exposes the underbelly of our actions, our inactions, and our trivialities.

We were feeding the homeless on the church property, and the city had issued us a cease and desist order. The neighborhood was up in arms over the fact that the "Other" was close to their homes. Fear was taking the driver's seat. It was a time of great turmoil and upheaval. One Sunday during this period of unrest, I was finishing up one service and getting ready for the next worshiping community. I was especially excited because we were confirming a group of youth. As I looked outside, I noticed the police had pulled up and called the leaders of the church to come to the parking lot. Two neighbors were putting flyers on the cars in our parking lot. The flyers contained inflammatory and harassing language about me and encouraged the congregation to rise up against their difficult pastor. One of the church members took a flyer off a car, and the neighbor called 911, stating that he was being accosted by a church member. They began a heated discussion, and the police showed up and tried to figure out what was going on. The neighbor accused the church member of assault. The member informed the

16

police that he had merely removed a flyer from his car and asked the neighbor to leave.

After quite a verbal scuffle, I walked with the officer to his car. I hadn't time to remove my clerical robes so, while I stood clothed in pastoral garb, the policeman railed at me about the church: "This is why I don't go to church, Pastor. Don't get me wrong: I believe in Jesus. But I don't believe the church acts like Jesus."

I apologized to the officer for the church's actions that day, and for the neighbors' actions. I explained that this was not what church was about. I told him we were sinners and that we often fall short, and I asked him to forgive us and to not take it out on Jesus. He drove away, and I felt my heart sink. I could just see Jesus turning over tables right there in the parking lot.

What needs to die in your church? That's where we start. We begin the journey of restarting your church by allowing for, even encouraging, places of death. We choose to have a memorial service for what worked in the past, to honor the prior period of time, and to make a decision to move forward. We choose to let the past set us free to fly, instead of letting the past become a shackle that chains us to a certain way of doing things.

Look around you with fresh eyes, and you will see obvious signs of the past still trying to shackle life in your church.

When a new pastor walks into a church that needs a restart, she or he walks into the setting with fresh eyes, ears, and nose. The first thing I see in reStart churches is clutter. Enormous amounts of clutter and disorganization. Clutter that looks like hoarding. In the midst of all the stuff from the past, I also notice no organization around the story of the past. There isn't a file or document I can read that tells the story of the church. There is nothing written down to remind new people who the members of the church have been on their journey or where God has met them.

In my current church, we spent my first year clearing out massive amounts of clutter. One day early in my tenure I walked into the nursery where the children are cared for during Sunday morning, and there was an aisle to walk through that led to a station with toys in the back of the room. The first thing I saw when I stepped into the room was a big sign that read "Do Not Come in Here without an adult!" I understood the sign because the area really was a danger zone. The "aisle" was actually a little path that cut through tall stacks of equipment, papers, toys, boxes, books, and papers. There was so much stuff crammed into the room, it was massively depressing. It was like four decades of children's activities were still living in this room. The problem was, there was no room for a child to play safely. I found there was only one child who came to this nursery, and truthfully, I was amazed that anyone would bring a child there. The past literally crowded people out.

Walking into a room greeted by a sign that begins with "Do Not" is just bad feng shui. It is a signpost of unwelcoming space. Each dying church I came to had signs that read "Do Not_____." They were written on 8x10 sheets of paper and plastered all over the church. In CrossRoads, my current church, there were signs posted on the cupboards in the kitchen, in the narthex where people first came into the building, and in the bathrooms.

When a new person walked into CrossRoads, they came into a cluttered narthex with junk everywhere. To the right was the sanctuary and to the left was the kitchen, visible as the heart of the church. The previous pastor told me on his exit, "Dottie, I know you're not going to believe it, but I've been working on getting the clutter out for a while, and we have made some progress. You see there is more to go."

18

One of the first things a newbie noticed was the kitchen. Unfortunately, there was a semiotic war going on in the kitchen between the preschool and the church. You could tell by the signs. On some cupboards was posted, "Do not touch! This belongs to the Preschool." And on other cupboards, "Do not use! This belongs to the Church."

I took a picture to remind me of the war in the kitchen, and the way that war was broadcast to the whole world. It is a picture of three cupboards with locks and huge chains on them to keep others locked out.

When I first saw the signs and the ridiculous, oversized chains—like you would use to lock down a barnyard door—on the kitchen cupboards, I called a meeting with the United Methodist Women, who seemed to own the kitchen, and the preschool. We discussed the signs and the space. I told them that we could share the space without a war, and that the signs and the chains and the locks must come down. They resisted. In fact, they questioned what would happen when someone stole from them. We decided that if either the church or the preschool took something from someone else's cupboard, we would replace it. I reminded everyone that this is a church, and that "Do not steal" is one of the Ten Commandments that I thought we could live by. I reminded everyone of how we live by grace and forgiveness when we err, and that there would be times when we erred. When this happened, we would talk, we would repair, and we would go on in relationship with one another in the kitchen.

So we took the signs down. And we took off the locks and the chains. It didn't solve the trust problem, but it was a start that made us aware we lived together.

A few months later, I walked into the kitchen to find the locks and the chains were back up on two of the church's cupboards. I asked the women who were meeting by the kitchen why the cupboards were locked again. They replied that they had to keep their good stuff locked up so no one else would use it. I reminded them that we agreed to no locks and chains in the kitchen. I asked the women to take them down. They answered me with a swift and definite "No!" Shocked by their reply, I invited them to unchain the cupboards before I had the opportunity to cut the chains off myself. I walked away.

One woman followed me out and nervously said, "Pastor, I know where the key is, and I will show you the key so you don't have to cut off the locks." She opened a drawer and showed me the key to the locks, saying, "Don't tell anyone I showed this to you."

Still a little stunned, and definitely curious, I unlocked the chained cabinets. What could be so precious in the lives of these women that it required a lock? I looked into the cabinets and saw paper products: paper plates, plastic utensils, and napkins. *This was worth a lock and key?* I thought. As I saw the cheap junk in the cabinets, something rose up in me, and I felt a spiritual longing to help souls that were locked shut in order to guard the stuff of life. This feeling was a mix of great sorrow and rising rage. Tears came to my eyes. The women were still meeting in the next room, but instead of going in to finish the conversation with them, I headed straight to my car and went home. So overwhelmed with emotion, I did not trust myself to be kind with my words, and so I went home to cry out to God: *God, what is going on here? Why do they cling to stuff?* God heard my upswell of emotions and received all my questions, and he allowed the sense of grief to stay for a while. I wasn't grieving the bad feng shui. I was grieving the spiritual emptiness I felt. God grieved over this church and signs that told the world, "Don't come here. We are still dealing with our stuff, and our souls aren't prepared for the newness of life. We aren't ready to share."

The incident reminds me of the story of Saul before he was made a king. Saul had gone looking for the family's lost donkeys when he had an encounter with God and the prophets. He was so moved that he began prophesying, and then he ran to the place where he could worship God. Overwhelmed by this experience, he lingered in worship, in the presence of God. Later he moved on. The prophet Samuel, meanwhile, was looking for the one who would be the new king. He went through all the tribes of Israel and landed on the family of Benjamin. Then he went through the Benjamite cousins until he landed on the family of Matri. And finally, he chose Saul, son of Kish, to be their new king. But when they looked for Saul, he was nowhere to be found. So they asked God where they could find Saul, and God's reply was, "He's hiding behind the baggage" (1 Samuel 10:22 NCV). They went to find Saul among the baggage, and they brought him out and celebrated the newly made king.

What I have found in the three churches that needed restarts is that they were hiding out among the baggage of their past. They were honoring their dead at the expense of their living.

As we began cleaning out the nursery, we found old vacation Bible school papers from four decades prior. While they were fascinating to see in a memorabilia sort of way, they weren't doing any good stacked in boxes and cluttered piles in the nursery. As we began throwing this stuff away, there was a lot of pain around letting it go. The people worried that they might need that curriculum, since it was expensive to buy new VBS materials. They thought perhaps we needed to store it somewhere, just in case it might be needed.

I pointed out, as I would many times in that first year, that we didn't have room to store anything in this church because every space was filled with stuff. They tackled that problem by stating we should go out and rent some storage space. I replied that we didn't need storage space, we needed to clean out this space, and we just might be amazed by how much usable room there actually would be.

They groaned, grieved, held tight, and fought as we all pried our fingers off the stuff of our history.

The book title *Does This Clutter Make My Butt Look Fat?*[1] gathers a wisdom that connects weight loss with decluttering. Peter Walsh found by accident that when people started getting rid of their clutter, they began to lose weight. And I'm wondering about the church as well. As we clean out the cobwebs of our past, will we become healthier, stronger, younger, and more spiritually whole?

Some churches may not have literal clutter but rather institutional or habitual clutter. "We've always done it this way" is a common statement about clutter. "I can't worship without my hymns, . . . my cross, . . . my pews" are declarations of a cluttered soul. The only One we worship is God. We don't worship our stuff, our memories, our dreams, our dashed hopes, or our traditions. We worship our God. We worship the one who knows how to raise up a king from a person who starts out hiding among the baggage.

There is hope for us. We may have surrounded ourselves with things that were once comforting and are now binding, but God still can choose us to lead the way forward. There's hope for clutter-dwellers, hoarders, and memory-storers. There's hope for the fearful ones who hold on with clenched hands, and there's hope for those who are in lockdown during a semiotic war in the kitchen. There's hope because God can make a way.

That is what I saw. What I saw was obvious to an outsider, but so familiar to the insider that it was not recognized. When I walked into my current setting, I spoke out, "It smells like 1960." The people looked at me like I had lost my mind and asked what I meant. I explained that, really, the smell in the place reminded me of 1960. Actually, that wasn't quite correct. What I smelled was the mustiness of a place closed up and cut off from fresh air, and that mustiness reminded me of a time of old, which for me was 1960. I'm sure 1960 didn't smell like this church smelled. But the area smelled like it hadn't experienced any fresh air since 1960. It was the smell of must, mold, and mildew. Things that happen when freshness is gone.

This is the state of many of our churches. They smell like a previous era. Literally, we smell staleness. And the outward sign of smell represents the inward sign of the spirit.

When we get married, we put on a ring and say, "This ring is an outward sign of an inward and spiritual grace, signifying to us the union between Jesus Christ and His church."[2]

The smells of our churches are outward signs of the spiritual state of our souls. And when we smell like a previous era, we announce to the world that we are living in the past. When people walk into our churches, the sign of smell speaks volumes to them. They don't have to talk to anyone to know that we reside in the past. Death has a smell. They smell it. They smell the rat, and they leave, never to come back again.

People can also hear our spiritual state. They hear our words of depression:

We don't have many young people, but we hope you'll come back.

Wow! It's so great to see you! (overly spoken as if they haven't seen a visitor in decades.)

We don't have any other children here, but we hope you will be our first.

Remember the words of remembrance called the Shema, which centered the people of Israel: "Israel, listen! Our God is the LORD! Only the LORD! Love the LORD your God with all your heart, all your being, and all your strength" (Deuteronomy 6:4-5).

The people were first admonished, encouraged to hear, to open up their ears to receive the sounds of the message. And the message was one of great love. Love God fully and wholly and completely. Love God with great strength.

When I was a little girl, I felt such a feeling of love well up in me when I hugged my mother that sometimes I squeezed her hard to express my great love. Loving God is like that. It's the big squeeze. It's the grand gesture. It is really hearing the message so that it soaks into our soul-space and transforms our outer space.

But instead, when we describe our churches, we speak out words that show the soul's depressed state. These words are sounds of hopelessness. We come at people, including ourselves, reminding everyone of our faults, as if we have no recognition of the beauty among us.

I have done this. I fight the urge to describe my church as an old congregation. That is what it was, but it is that no more. And before it became a multigenerational place of gathering, we had to take a leap of faith and describe our reality as if it were already here. That feels weird and almost like we are telling a fable. But faith requires hearing, and hearing requires faith in God. When we speak, what story do we tell ourselves, and others? Is it the story of our failings, or the story of how God met us in our failure and showed something new and beautiful among us?

What is your church beautiful at? Does it sound beautiful when it sings? Is it beautiful in community? Is it a beautiful place for mission? What is your church's beauty, and how can you shout out the good, while changing the not-so-good?

The world doesn't come into our sanctuaries much anymore, though I hear they really do want to worship with us. They just don't like what they see, smell, and hear. And so the world worships where they can: at concerts, at nationally televised funerals, and in nature. These are good places to worship, because anywhere God is, that is a good place to worship God. But we have a history of worship that people are looking for. When they are distracted by our outward signs, they cannot see, hear, or smell our inward love. And so we must regain our position of beauty. It is not a position of power, success, or numerical significance. It is a position of ashes, death, service, humility, and great grace. This is our beauty, and it is time to speak it out.

Unfortunately, we are so busy declining we don't have time to feed the sheep. John Flowers and Karen Vannoy state that some churches really don't have any reason to grow, and in fact, have positioned themselves for decline on purpose! They list these reasons as "incentives for decline":

1. The individual member becomes more powerful the smaller the church.

2. The church feels more intimate and familiar as it declines. Also, not much is happening, so it's easier to stay informed.

3. The growing sense of familiarity and intimacy also makes the church feel more caring.

4. While youth and children's programs are the first to decline in numbers, fewer numbers provide for less disruption in worship, less pressure for change, and ease the strain on budgets and volunteers.

5. Fewer people make assimilation less work. As church growth ceases, members can spend more time visiting with existing friends, which is more fun and enjoyable anyway.

6. The church as a place of safety becomes primary over the risk of following Jesus. Just as some people live in a gated community to keep the world out, some church members feel safer with a symbolic gate around the church too.

7. Finally, members with limited gifts and graces for leadership now find themselves in leadership positions. Sometimes they are asked to fill multiple offices, and feel indispensable. The ill-suited leaders can become resistant to losing this recognition and power.[3]

When you look at the church God has placed you in at this moment, are you set for decline or straining for a new start? Have things become so easy that the modus operandi of your setting is a slow, drawn-out decline? It is time to face the reality of our situations, to stop lying to ourselves, and to be bold enough and trusting enough to take a step toward God's way of being the church. Since the foundation of the church is death and resurrection, it is now that we begin. The possibilities are endless when we give in to what must die, and when we look for the spaces and places that God inhabits.

First, look for the places of death. I know this is an unpopular idea because we love to hang on to and protect what is struggling in our midst, but if we are to live out the Christian story, we must also invite death into our midst. Where are you dying, and how can you allow for death to occur naturally, quickly, and with honor?

Death might occur naturally in a variety of settings. If your congregation has an average age of eighty or more, and your numbers are dwindling at the same rates as the natural deaths in your midst, then you are dying. If new people do not become a part of your community on a regular basis, then you are dying, because life requires new disciples of Christ. If you do not have baptisms, or members who join by a profession of faith in Jesus Christ, then you are dying. If people come to church because it is their habit but they lack a passion for serving Jesus Christ, if your members are more concerned about the music than they are about the praise, if the battles are inward and not outward, then your church is dying.

Pay attention to the dying places. Honor them for the work of their past. Allow for that death to speak to you and assist you in seeing your present. Either we can pretend death is not near (many people who are gravely ill do this), or we can look at it and allow death to propel us to new life. Revelation reminds us of this: "Wake up and strengthen whatever you have left, teetering on the brink of death, for I've found that your works are far from complete in the eyes of my God. So remember what you received and heard. Hold on to it and change your hearts and lives" (Revelation 3:2-3). Death both propels us and strengthens us for the work of new life. And yet we run from the event and the lesson the event brings us.

We resist beauty when we resist the death that must occur. Mustiness is a sign of lack of airflow. And the fresh wind of the Holy Spirit is the sign of a movement of God. The hard thing is to allow death with honor to become part of our story, and to give in to it by releasing our need to control and instead trusting God in everything. This is the hard work of the church. It is also what makes us beautiful, truthful, and good. When we die, God rises in our place, and the people of the world get to see God among us. As this happens, we become naturally invitational, hospitable, and welcoming. God's grace is attractive. Our humility in the face of death is the requirement.

An e-mail popped up from our nursery caregiver, Gina. "Pastor," she wrote, "we have a problem in the nursery." Gina described how we have too many children there and need more workers to assist her. The nursery has grown and is filled with beautiful infants and toddlers who fill the space with joy, laughter, and the kind of love that only a child can know. After I read the e-mail, I got up and did a boogie-woogie dance of joy in my office. God is so great that blessings come in the middle of the dying places.

Where are you dying? Lean into that death. God is waiting to take residence in our dying and in God's rising among us.

THREE

THE WILD, WILD WEST

reCognize

Growing up in Nogales, Arizona, on the border of Mexico, I was enamored with the stories of the Wild West. Men and women climbed into covered wagons and came out West, looking for a new start. They traveled through tough weather and through wilderness without roads. They headed in a future direction, seeking a territory they had never traversed. Travelers journeyed from pine trees to cactus to orange orchards to ocean. They went over flatlands and beautiful sloping hills and treacherous mountains as they searched for the rumored sea on the other side of their world. Many nights were spent around a fire, trying to keep warm, taking comfort in the beauty of the bright moon, and feeling fearful when the coyotes howled. They bathed in the streams and washed their clothes in the rivers. They kept going when their wagons failed them, when the weather nailed them, and when they couldn't see how far they had to go. They had a dream, and they didn't stop, didn't turn around, and didn't falter in their belief that there was a new home and a new way of living out there. Along the way, some of these wagoners lost their sons and daughters. Some lost their mothers, fathers, sisters, and brothers. Some lost dear friends. They were grounded for a time by grief, but then they buried their beloved dead, said their prayers, and they moved on, slowly at first, but gradually with regained confidence and speed.

They weren't the only ones on the trails of the Wild West. Native Americans were trying to keep their sacred lands holy. Mexicans, who had lived here for centuries, were suddenly pushed out of power. The land was filled with people struggling to live in their own way and struggling to survive during a time of major transition. Wars, power struggles, loss, and pain were central themes as the land groaned under the weight of change. It wasn't easy for anyone.

Perhaps you've seen movies about the towns that were newly formed. You remember the gunfights, the barroom brawls, and how law was not based on order or justice. Mid-twentieth-century filmmakers provide us with a vivid imagination of women ushering their children quickly across the street so they wouldn't catch a stray bullet. Or we saw old men peeking out from the bar, hoping that things had calmed down enough for them to stagger home. And yet the people pulled together to build one another's homes and businesses, a church and the school in the center of the square. Teachers were sought after and well cared for—they filled a tender and precious role that was valued in the middle of the wildness of their towns. Everything was new, yet they figured out how to bring a little form to the lack of structure in their lives. They worked together to survive. They were close and interdependent in a world where nothing made much sense. They began to create a new way of life.

As a little girl, I wondered what it would be like to tackle a frontier, to explore unknown territory, to know adventure and pain. I fantasized about being a Wild West woman, though my world was really tame. I thought there must be something of the courage and strength of those pioneers left inside of me. After all, I grew up on the same ground that they had walked on. The same spirit of the sacred space of the Native Americans and the same blood of the Mexicans coursed through my veins. I could feel their boldness, and I hoped to be like them someday.

Such thoughts from a very shy young girl! I couldn't muster enough courage to speak up at the grocery store because the woman behind the counter was a "stranger." I'd just slide the money her way, give her my smile, and hope that she wouldn't speak to me. In school I was known as the one who didn't say much. Courage was not on my list of obvious characteristics. But the imagination is a wonderful thing! I could imagine something happening in me that seemed unimaginable to most. I could see myself dressed in boots and a hat, wearing a serape for warmth and riding a beautiful paint mustang as I scouted out the trail ahead of the wagons, looking across landscapes so the makeshift road could be traversed in safety. I never saw myself riding the wagon, only my horse. Sometimes I would imagine that I was fighting alongside the Native Americans and leading a battle for the sacred land. And sometimes I found myself in the middle of a little Mexican community, laughing and dancing around the pushed-back tables as we told stories and tended to our wounds.

The place where I was born, and the cultural stories that shaped my imagination, have informed my present day and my present role: pastor to dwindling American congregations. Most of us see the church today set in a culture of great transition, an unknown territory through which we must travel. We each need the spirit of the Wild West frontier to flow through our veins in order to find our way to a future, even though there is no road, no road map, and no GPS. It is time for the scouts, today called "futurists," to focus on the horizon of Jesus' church, and to call out the obstacles, best directions, and possibilities. It is time to call for the courage of the pioneers to resurface in our congregations, because a different outcome is available to those who want to restart their ministry.

Remember the story of Moses, who sent out twelve men, leaders of the tribes, to scout out the land of Canaan and come back with a report? The men went ahead to search the land and came back with two reports. Ten of the leaders stated,

> "We entered the land to which you sent us. It's actually full of milk and honey, and this is its fruit. There are, however, powerful people who live in the land. The cities have huge fortifications. And we even saw the descendants of the Anakites there. The Amalekites live in the land of the arid southern plain; the Hittites, Jebusites, and Amorites live in the mountains; and the Canaanites live by the sea and along the Jordan." (Numbers 13:27-29).

But two of the leaders, Caleb and Joshua, had a different slant on the report. Caleb attempted to calm their fears by saying, "We must go up and take possession of it, because we are more than able to do it" (Numbers 13:30). Only two of the twelve had faith in God's ability to call, direct, and make a way.

Then it got worse! The ten men expanded their report in the negative:

> But the men who went up with him said, "We can't go up against the people because they are stronger than we." They started a rumor about the land that they had

explored, telling the Israelites, "The land that we crossed over to explore is a land that devours its residents. All the people we saw in it are huge men. We saw there the Nephilim (the descendants of Anak come from the Nephilim). We saw ourselves as grasshoppers, and that's how we appeared to them." (Numbers 13:31-33)

They started a rebellion against their leaders, rabble-rousing among the people. They stirred up the people in fear. It wasn't too hard to do. Moses and Aaron fell on their faces to pray. And at the same time, Joshua and Caleb ripped their clothes to show their great grief at what they were hearing, and they encouraged the people with these words:

"The land we crossed through to explore is an exceptionally good land. If the LORD is pleased with us, he'll bring us into this land and give it to us. It's a land that's full of milk and honey. Only don't rebel against the LORD and don't be afraid of the people of the land. They are our prey. Their defense has deserted them, but the LORD is with us. So don't be afraid of them." (Numbers 14:7-9)

The people were so into their fear that they plotted to stone the ones who spoke out in faith and trust in God. The story describes how God got angry at those who allowed their fears to stop them from fulfilling their purpose in the Promised Land.

Scouts on the frontier are those who tell the truth through the lens of trust in God. Today we need more scouts, those who go ahead and point the way with faithfulness and courage.

We need scouts because the church is in a "heap of trouble." In 2009 Rev. Adam Hamilton said that if we continue in our current course of events, The United Methodist Church will be dead in forty-four years.[1]

Using current population projections, Lovett H. Weems Jr. states that the church will be greatly affected by a coming death tsunami, which will begin to crest in 2018.[2] We are in a state of wilderness whether we recognize it or not. You've read the statistics, and you know as well as I do that your pews are not full and your neighborhood is not coming to your door as they once did. We see that the world has changed around us, and we don't quite know what to do about it. The cosmic groan of the church is being heard around the world.

We can do better.

The Church Needs to ReCognize

I'm continually amazed that I've been a pastor in churches that were, and are, in the midst of a turnaround. My limited imagination always put me in growing, healthy megachurches with no financial difficulties. I never prayed for this. I've had to learn to be a new person and to let loose of some old ideas in order to walk with a church that needed a major change. Most of the time, I realized that no rulebook or guidebook was adequate for driving this paradigm shift. Admittedly, I failed and faltered, then got up and continued walking, until I began to learn. There is no map except the road of faith, and every road is different, and every church unique.

The truth is, we don't usually get to choose how to restart our churches. We can make a plan, but usually God has another plan. I suggest that we follow God's plan. It may look crazy. It might not make sense. But when it is God's plan, it is much better than ours.

To recognize is to think again. *Cognition* means

1. The mental process of knowing, including aspects such as awareness, perception, reasoning, and judgment.

34

2. That which comes to be known, as through perception, reasoning, or intuition; knowledge.[3]

To recognize is also to see again. When we see someone we recognize, we remember our connection or previous meeting. We know that we know that person. Sometimes we even recognize someone when we can't recall her or his name. It is the same way with the church. Something inside you will recognize the genuine church when you encounter it. As you stumble forward, there will be an "aha!" moment when you recall some deep, even guttural, understanding of rightness. Keep looking for what you know to be true.

Name the Curses and the Blessings

A place to re-know our church is in understanding the places of cursing and blessing. As God presents the Ten Commandments to Moses, God stops to explain the consequences of our actions:

> Do not bow down to them or worship them, because I, the LORD your God, am a passionate God. I punish children for their parents' sins even to the third and fourth generations of those who hate me. But I am loyal and gracious to the thousandth generation of those who love me and keep my commandments. (Exodus 20:5-6)

The consequence of our sin is that our children, grandchildren, and great-grandchildren suffer for our actions. If you have ever worked in the field of child abuse, you know that the pattern of hurt can easily be passed on. We see the results of one parent's abusive behavior continuing on through the family line.

The tendency to act in the way that is familiar is the hardest thing to break. Perhaps you've had a moment when you said to yourself, *I sound just like my mother!* and that statement doesn't

35

seem so wonderful. You say the thing to your children that you swore as a child you would never say. Pain is passed on easily. God recognizes this passing on by saying the punishment for our sin is carried on. We could, of course, debate whether or not God is the great punisher, but then we miss the point of this passage. It notes the consequence of our sin, and the consequence is personal and familial. But the next breath-of-words tells the whole picture: God is loyal and loving to the thousandth family line when we follow God and love God's ways. Personally, I don't think of God as the great punisher but rather the Great Lover. The consequences of sin in this scripture are overwhelmingly diminished by the continuance of love. Do you not see it?

Humanly, we focus on the curse. Heavenly, we feel the blessing.

But our churches have learned to focus on the curse. We know the story of our decline like we know the smell of our lover's breath. It is so familiar that we reject any change that might bring a sweeter smell. Walking into restart churches, the first stories we hear are the ones of the curse. We hear which pastors destroyed the church, and which lay leaders saved the church from these pastors at great personal peril.

When I was in kindergarten, my family moved to Laredo, Texas, where I first began learning Spanish. Dad's first language is Spanish, so when I learned a phrase I would excitedly run home to ask Dad what it meant. The first phrases I learned were the ones that had the best vocal emphasis. And as I asked Dad what they meant, we saw a pattern developing. My first phrases were swearwords and phrases. Dad patiently told me the meaning of each of those words and phrases, but he was relieved when my Spanish developed enough that there was no more swearing. The first things we hear are the worst things, because that is what we emphasize.

For example, we hear about the big, bad denomination that requires "taxation" with nothing in return. In the Methodist tradition, this translates to: "They expect us to pay apportionments when they keep sending us pastors from hell."

The assumption is that the curse of denominational expectations is worked out in a formula called "tit for tat." The expression "tit for tat" means more than an exchange; rather, it means the deeper idea of blow for blow, as with a fistfight.[4] It is more like, "You send us a bad pastor (punch-in-the-face), and we'll stop paying your salary and your missionaries (punch-in-the-gut)." We rely on the back-and-forth curses to keep us distracted from the work at hand: loving God and our neighbors as ourselves (Matthew 22:37-40). Yet we follow the Christ who said when someone hits you in the face, turn the other cheek to them also (Matthew 5:39).

In each reStart church I have served, I have heard stories of evil, pain, and abuse. The stories are similar: "We had a heyday when I was young, and everything was perfect. Then that pastor left, and we had a series of pastors. Some were fair, and others were awful. One pastor destroyed us. We now distrust the whole denomination, and we aren't sure you are any better, Pastor, but we sure hope you can save us!" The story is the same, and the details of arguments, fights, and frustrations make for a great burning ceremony. It is as if the congregations choose to remain in places of purposeful pain forever. This is not usually a conscious choice, but a patterned reaction.

What is your church cursed with? Hint: Your stories will give you the answer.

How can you go about breaking the curse?

Churches are also carriers of generational blessings. Unfortunately, it is sometimes hard to find the blessings underneath all of the curses.

But since God promised blessings to the thousandth generation, your church is filled with blessings. Even if you have to dig deep to find them, the burrowing is well worth the effort.

At Liberty United Methodist Church, I found a strong group of people who trained pastors and sent them out with great pride, fully expecting that some of them would change the world for the better in different locations. At Mission Bell United Methodist Church, I found a church that had the courage to take risks no matter the cost, for they understood the cost of Christ is to die in order to live. They rarely fought necessary change. At CrossRoads United Methodist Church, I found a congregation steeped in formation around feeding the hungry. They also knew how to sing softly.

The first time I went to CrossRoads before being assigned there, I snuck in to check them out. Sitting in the back of the sanctuary, I cried out to God, because I didn't like the thought of taking on an aging congregation. It was not in my bag of dreams. So I asked God to show me what they were good at. Right there in the service, I closed my eyes and heard them sing. They didn't sing with gusto, or even with fanfare, but they sang with the soft strength of ones who knew the meaning behind each word. I knew God was already at work in ways I couldn't yet see.

Even now, in the traditional service, when I sit up front, I close my eyes so that I can hear the singing from behind me. The voices wash over my soul and minister to this minister so that I can minister back. This is one of their blessings. After I arrived, we started another worshiping community that praises and sings with great abandon, in a different style that speaks to a different group. And that too is beautiful. I have a sense that generations will sing God's praises because this generation chose to sing. And I have a sense that hungry people will be fed for generations, even to the thousandth generation, because they have made feeding the hungry a priority.

Sometimes we have to stop and re-know what we think we know and re-think what we bless and what we curse.

In order to re-think our blessings, we must find the places that God inhabits. God, for example, inhabits the praise of the people. Where are the praises? God inhabits the hearts of those who seek to follow God. Where are the seekers? God promises presence to the outcasts, the left-behinds, and the poor of our society. Where are they living?

I received a letter from a woman who gives life to the future of the church. Her name is Mary. She had heard through the news that we were working with the homeless, and she sent me a long letter one day, telling me about her life. Mary lives outdoors behind a small strip mall. She lives on the pavement. She had begun to meet and help out the owners of the businesses around her. She runs off people who try to break in during the night. Mary weighs all of about eighty pounds, but she has a two-hundred-pound voice when she wants to use it. They call her "the bull-dog." I think of her as being like a Chihuahua: a little woman who doesn't know she is small and takes on the world to protect those she loves.

The shopkeepers had begun to take care of Mary, because she was taking care of them. One of them put a shed out back, and Mary now has a "house" to live in. She calls the police when there is trouble, and they are now her protectors. She cleans towels for the nail salon, and they give her soup. She cried when the restaurant owner's wife died and attended her funeral, sitting in the back for fear of being ostracized. The owner brought her near the front in love. She cares for her little spot on this planet, and she is loved.

When I stop by Mary's back alley, I ask her what she needs. "Nothing, Pastor! I'm fine!" she usually says. "Thanks for checking on me though." We talk. Mary comes to the church only to deliver me letters. Her letters tell me the story of her life. As soon as she hands me a letter,

Mary leaves, because she is still not sure she is welcome. She has never attended our worship services, but she is one of ours. She considers me her pastor. God inhabits her, and she praises God daily for the goodness she sees in her life.

Mary is where God is.

In our churches we need to seek out new places, new people groups, and the new movement of the Holy Spirit. The Holy Spirit is always a breath of fresh air. It is not stale, dry, or dead. When we feel the wind blowing, and we follow it, we are looking for God's presence in the newness of life. And out of that, a movement for recognizing Jesus in our midst will begin.

Author and entrepreneur Seth Godin believes that every person can create a micromovement, and that all that is needed is a little move of faith. The five things to do in a micromovement are:

1. Publish a manifesto.
2. Make it easy for your followers to connect with you.
3. Make it easy for your followers to connect with one another.
4. Realize that money is not the point of a movement.
5. Track your progress.[5]

Churches have published vision statements, goals, and strategic plans, but a manifesto is for the world to know what the church is up to. Like Martin Luther's Ninety-five Theses, what would your church nail to the front door (or post to the Internet) for the world to see? At the same time, working on connections between seekers is one of the main reasons for discipleship. Together, the church can grow in faith. Alone, a church member just feels alone. Social media is the new front-door communication tool for ongoing discipleship, and it can leap over the wall of our busy lifestyles, bringing daily and weekly posts into our homes.

ReCognize Pioneer Faith

Our pioneering hope is based on our collective story, which is the story of resurrection from the dead! Jesus rose above death. He set it behind him and forged ahead with life. And we are called to do the same: to face down our death and move to life.

You know the death curses around you. You know the last-breath events in your setting. You know the smell of endings that you live with. The author of our faith is a God wild enough to bring hope and life in the dead and near-dead places of our churches and our lives. That's the factor that gives us faith in our future and the ability to work through our present. God's grace constrains us to keep trying to live and to keep searching for the way of life. Not because of pride or territorialism or tradition or history, but because the good news is still meant for every person and because we are still called to be gospel-deliverers and way-walkers.

There is a wild pioneer scout and a wild church inside of you. And God can use your imagination for a greater future, to make a dream come true in your church. I believe this because I know what God has done in me, and when I see God at work in this sacred space of my life, the transformation brings me the joy that sets my feet to dancin'.

I hope you recognize your courage. I hope you feel encouraged. I hope you are one of the pioneers of the new wild frontier of the church. Come on. . . . I can't fully see the way, though I know it's out there, but we pioneers won't be the same without your voice and your wisdom on the journey.

WILLING HEART, NOT LEADERSHIP

reAlize

Perhaps you've read your share of books on leadership. I have learned a lot about how to lead, including things no one else took the time to tell me and things I failed to hear along the way, from the books I've read and the people I've followed. But sometimes I take the unintended leap and think if I follow a perfectly prescribed series of steps for leading well, my church will succeed. Which means, all I need is to be more charismatic, more organized, more team-oriented, and more of this or that. The demands of the leadership agenda leave us feeling overwhelmed when we look at the limitations of our gifts, and the chasm between who we are and who we need to be to lead well.

Restarting your ministry is not all about leadership. It's about other stuff too. Remember the calling. God chose *you* for ministry in your church setting. You may be shaking in your bare feet like Moses, wondering why you were chosen. But that doesn't matter much. God knows your lack of self-confidence and called you anyway. God didn't call us because we had it all together. God called us because God *can*. There's no formula to who gets called into this field. It doesn't have to make sense. It just is.

My favorite Bible story of a called leader is that of Gideon. Gideon really wasn't leadership material. He was in the smallest clan, and in his clan, he was considered to be bottom-rung material. All he cared about was finding a little wheat for his hungry family in a time of great trouble. The Midianites, Amalekites, and people of the East were marauding across the land, stealing the crops that the people had grown and taking them for their troops. They stole sheep, oxen, and donkeys. They came in hordes, thick as locusts, riding on camels that spit out meanness, and they stripped the land bare. They left Gideon's people desolate, hungry, and hopeless.

But Gideon found some wheat left over from the marauding hordes and hid out in the bottom of the winepress, hoping to make flour to feed his family. He must've been scared to death down there. He must've wondered if he'd be caught and taken away, or if he'd be able to get some food into the mouths of his hungry family. He certainly didn't feel courage. Just fear.

And into his pit of fear an angel appeared and said to him, "Mighty hero, the LORD is with you!" (Judges 6:12 NLT).

I wonder if Gideon looked around in the winepress to see if there were any others there that he hadn't noticed, because he certainly didn't feel like a "hero." Then he realized that the angel was talking to him. And he argued with the angel, saying, "If the LORD is with us, why has all this happened to us? And where are all the miracles our ancestors told us about? Didn't they say, 'The LORD brought us up out of Egypt'? But now the LORD has abandoned us and handed us over to the Midianites" (Judges 6:13 NLT).

Did you ever feel like Gideon in your setting? The enemies of church life surround you. The culture has abandoned religion, and the few people you have left are working hard with too few results. We wonder what we are doing in these places, and we cry out to God to save us, and when we don't hear an answer, we begin to doubt, perhaps saying, "Those miracles that I heard about when I went to that last big church conference, miracles of a full and overbrimming house, miracles of lives being turned around, miracles of financial stability . . . they didn't translate to my neighborhood."

We wonder if we have been abandoned by our society, by our denominational system, or even by our God. After all, God is the one who put us here! So we argue with God. We pray and we try to keep up with the times by ordering computers and projectors and by creating websites, but really, no one notices these minor technological changes. Was it money and time well spent?

Len Sweet recalls the work of Warren G. Bennis and Richard J. Thomas, saying that it's more about "voice" than "charisma" when it comes to leadership.[1]

It's not the power of the "charisma" that makes the difference. It's the power of voice. It's the development of an inner ear trained to trust and to try the inner voice.[2]

Sweet says that our voice has these components:

1. It tells the truth.

2. It promotes social justice and spiritual vibrancy.

3. It generates original sounds.

4. It speaks from experience.[3]

Sometimes I think we have lost our voices. We are bombarded with the noise of our culture, and we are so in tune with the voices around us that we can't hear our own sounds. We don't realize the power of our own voices.

God created your uniqueness and gave you a voice. Your voice may not be the one some want to hear, but it is still your voice. Your voice may sound different from voices of the past, but it is still your voice. Your voice may vibrate on a different plane of musicality, but it is still your voice.

I remember a time in my first years of ministry that a gentleman came to me and said that he had trouble listening to my voice. I asked him why, and he said, "Well, Pastor, your voice is soft and not hard; it is high and not deep. And you are a woman, and I have a hard time hearing the message of Jesus from a woman."

I thought to myself but didn't say out loud, *Some things I can't change—like my gender!* I knew from talking to this man that my being a woman was difficult for him. He liked me personally, but he didn't like me in the pulpit. He was nice enough about it, but former conversations had shown that he wouldn't be changing his view anytime soon.

So I said, "Well, my friend, there are many wonderful, deep, strong, male voices that you can hear in the pulpits of this town. We will miss you, but you need to find someone you can hear." He left our church, occasionally visiting to hear me one more time. Teehee! God chuckled every time the man visited our church.

Not everyone can hear your kind of voice, but that doesn't mean you are to abandon it. Your voice is your voice. It doesn't belong to anyone else. God can speak to certain people only through you, and that's why you were created in your own uniqueness.

One of the problems with our churches is that we have abandoned our original voices. Like Gideon, we are hiding out in the wine vat, bowled over by the criticisms that fly our way, shackled by the need to please and make everyone happy, and silenced by our fear of being fully used for God's glory. Sweet reminds us, "Nothing sinks a ship faster than negativity."[4]

That sinking ship adds weight when its leaders believe the negative voices in their community, allowing negativity to shut down the power of their unique voices. Walking in the role of "pastor" means that you have a target on your back fairly frequently. The arrows are not usually substantial, but petty rumblings of discontent. People will try to wrestle away your uniqueness in an attempt to take over your role of leadership. They don't usually mean to, and they don't usually know what they are doing, but the effect of the wrestling can leave you reluctant to speak out the words God gives you, because you know the trouble that will come when you open up the mouth that is connected to the heart of God. That is just the way it is.

To top off the negative voices, there is the fact that most of our churches are in actual decline. Maybe the decline is rapid and sudden, or maybe it has been in process over many years, moving so slowly that the people are used to it and don't even see the death in their midst. Either way, the naysayers are joined in by the fact-finding voice of the current state. Our churches have gone downhill, and we have been witness to the slippery slope. Maybe you can see the decline around you, or maybe the recognition is still new and near.

Jim Collins writes in *How the Mighty Fall: And Why Some Companies Never Give In*, that there are five stages of decline. The story of business decline can also be utilized to understand the precarious state the church may be in. The stages are:

1. Hubris Born of Success. This happens when arrogance and pride step in, often born of success. Organizations begin to rely on past success as indicators for the same in the present arena.

2. Undisciplined Pursuit of More. When success causes one to reach out for more, the temptation to grow larger is actualized. However, it is also possible to grow large without sufficient support structures.

3. Denial of Risk and Peril. Here leaders use positive talk to ignore bleak facts.

4. Grasping for Salvation. Now, a sharp decline cannot be ignored. They begin to look outside for a "savior" to stop the flow of decline.

5. Capitulation to Irrelevance or Death. A run of problems brings hopelessness and abandonment.[5]

So what is our response to decline and death? What can we do when our opponents' voices are loud and clear? How do we start the change?

Realize. When God chose you to lead, God didn't give you an adaptive voice; God gave you a particular voice. It is up to you to realize (make actual) the strength, power, and compassion that reside within your voice. Your particular vocality is connected to God's message, and if the vibrations of your sound are not heard around the world, someone will not get the chance to know God's love. Someone will be lost. Someone will remain hopeless. Someone will die of a broken heart. Make your voice true to who God made you to be.

Remember, in the biblical story the angel decidedly called Gideon a "mighty hero"! Gideon, the one without courage. Gideon, the one playing "hide-and-don't-seek." Gideon, the one voted "Least Likely to Succeed" by his clan. "Hero? Me?"

It's as if the angel called out of Gideon something that he didn't know he had within him. He called out courage, strength, and a can-try attitude. And Gideon was told that all he had to do was take what he already had, and that would be enough to save him and his people. Gideon didn't recognize the gifts that he had, but the angel did. The Lord called him to his strength, saying, "Go with the strength you have, and rescue Israel from the Midianites. I am sending you!" (Judges 6:14 NLT).

When the Lord proclaimed, "I am sending you!" I wonder if the emphasis was on the "I," meaning, "God is on your side so you don't have to worry," or on the "you!" meaning, "Yes, it's really you that has been called."

Gideon doesn't give up easily on his self-doubt. He tells the angel that he's from the clan of Manasseh, which everyone knows is the weakest clan of all. And that in his clan, he's really scum, a nobody, a bottom-feeder. But the Lord reminds him, "I will be with you. And you will destroy the Midianites as if you were fighting against one man" (Judges 6:16 NLT).

In other words, "It will be easier than you think! You're not alone, buddy." So often we think that the task is overwhelming because we mistakenly believe we are doing it alone, with only our strength, our limited time, and our small set of talents. And while it is good to know our limitations, it is not so good to live by them. Our limitations are only the lines we must cross in faith.

When we come to a border—a limit in our lives, a line drawn in the sand—in order to step over, we must have faith in God. It is then that we put in operation what we have said we believe all along. When we step over in faith, trusting that God is up to something in our lives, then we are privileged to see God work. Often, when we take that step of faith, we don't see immediate results. But that is part of the mystery of faith. Things may be happening in God's sphere of the world that we don't see. But faith is faith, and it does not necessitate visual effects. Instead, God works, and sometimes we see the results, sometimes we feel the results, and sometimes we get to keep believing that the results are in process.

To call on the fact that we are not alone is the greatest strength that we have. We are never alone. "Separate," "independent," and "solo" are not tools in our toolbox. "Connected," "interdependent," "together"— these are the tools Christ-followers choose to utilize. Remember that God is at work always, and when God works, we are bonded together in awe.

But what if you believe that, and want to act that way, but don't have the maturity to take such a radical stand? For example, your child has gone down a path that you don't understand. She has been taught right and loved well, and you have told her of her beauty, but somewhere on the journey of her life, she got confused and she chose to live a life of ugliness and degradation. What do you do? Do you wallow in misery because she is miserable, because of your pain? Do you call her names, get angry, push her away with your hurt? All those are natural reactions to pain, but we choose to live in faith, and so we call her "beautiful," and we tell her that we believe in her and know she will find her way, and we remind her that we are there for her and always praying for her. And we remind her that our love for her will never die. When we stand in that place of faith, our daughters, and our sons, will eventually choose their healing.

What if your church is dying as you read this page? Your congregants are in their eighties, and while we live longer these days, this still puts you in a setting where death is within a decade. What if there are more empty pews than full? What do you do? By faith, you preach every Sunday to the saints you can see and to the saints you can't see. By faith, you speak to your people about those folk who are coming into your church—people of all ages, races, and nations. By faith you find your niche, believe in it, and work it until it is working on its own. You keep on believing because that is what you were called to do. And you call on your team of eighty-year-olds, asking for their prayers for the next generation; and you call on your pastor friends, asking for their wisdom; and you call on your community around your church, asking for understanding of their needs. By faith you remember that you are surrounded by the saints who came before you and by the saints who will come after you.

You become the reluctant and surprising hero. Not because you deserve it, but because God put you in your place to eke out the bread of life from what is left of your church. Even though you may be hiding away in the choir room, God is still able to find you and call you out to the coffeehouse to save the day. Most of us don't want to be called heroes. It makes us squirm in our flip-flops. But God didn't promise us that we'd be comfortable; just that we'd be called and surrounded by God's forces. And the thing that God asked Gideon, and that perhaps God is asking you, is "Are you willing?" Note the question is not "Are you able?" just "Are you willing?" You may have innate leadership gifts, or you may have developed leadership gifts over time, but that's really not the point! Are you willing to step out of the wine barrel and lead your motley group of church folk into the world that has changed so that the gospel of Jesus Christ can still be heard?

A story about Winston Churchill recalls that in the late 1920s, he had fallen into deep despair.[6] He was in his late fifties, his body was failing him (less hair and more weight), and he was taking the blame for Great Britain's financial problems. He split with his political party and created a hole of isolation around himself. He even refused to meet with Gandhi during his hiding period. The 1929 stock market crash brought Churchill financial failure, and during that same time, he was hit by a car in New York (he looked the wrong way!) and ended up in the hospital with a long recovery time ahead of him. Churchill was depressed.

When Joseph Stalin asked Lady Astor about Winston Churchill's state, Lady Astor quickly quipped, "Oh, he's finished."

From a historical perspective, things looked different. It was, in fact, a short eight years later that Winston Churchill stood before his Parliament as prime minister and spoke life and breath into the despairing situation of a world controlled by Hitler and Nazism, saying,

> We shall never surrender, and even if, which I do not for a moment believe, this Island or a large part of it were subjugated and starving, then our Empire beyond the seas, armed and guarded by the British Fleet, would carry on the struggle, until, in God's good time, the New World, with all its power and might, steps forth to the rescue and the liberation of the old.[7]

The end of the story of Churchill's rise to become one of the world's most influential leaders occurs at a commencement ceremony for his alma mater, Harrow. He had been a student who earned very low grades, an embarrassment of sorts. And on the day of the ceremony, Churchill slept his way through the event. But when it was his turn to speak, Winston Churchill got up to the podium and spoke out these famous words of advice to the graduates: "This is the lesson: never give in, never give in, never, never, never, never—in nothing great or small, large or petty—never give in except to convictions of honour and good sense. Never yield to force; never yield to the apparently overwhelming might of the enemy."[8]

Churchill learned in life to keep on going despite desperate situations.

One of the greatest surprises of my life occurred when I was sent to Mission Bell United Methodist Church in Phoenix. The place looked like it was dead: unmowed brown grass, paint chipping away, clutter everywhere. Inside the church were a group of people who knew that the church was not going to survive very long if things continued as they were. We had a conversation, and they told me that they were willing to do whatever they needed to do to live and to be alive in this place. So we went to work. We mowed the lawn and painted the building and cut down the dead trees. We repaired the broken bell in the tower so it could actually ring, which meant un-sticking the clapper that had been welded to the inside of the bell (now, that's a metaphor of death: don't ring out the good news!).

The first thing we did was look at our current state full in the face by admitting what we were and what we hoped to change. We changed out leadership positions and streamlined the administrative boards and process. We learned to laugh together and work together. We welcomed in children who broke the water main and ran through the worship center with abandon, much to our delight and the trustees' consternation. After the water pipe broke and water was spewing all over the dust and dirt behind the education building, a trustee came running to me, breathlessly spewing, "Pastor, the children broke the water main! What should we do?" This was the first event at which we'd had actual children in our church for many years, so we had been celebrating their presence. I turned to Mr. Trustee and said, "Well, now, isn't that a great problem to have?" (We could not have this problem without children around.) And then I smiled my sweetest smile and said, "I guess we (the royal 'we' that really means 'you') need to fix it!"

We watched God come alongside us and take the seeds of our efforts and make something beautiful grow. We became one another's heroes, much to our surprise. It was five and a half years of learning to be a church that went from hiding out to ringing out the good news to our neighborhood. We thrived again, thanks to a God who made something mighty of our minor efforts. We experienced the actualization of our hopes on Bell Road.

We have believed that our gifts and talents are needed by God in order to spread the gospel. But that is a lie. God can, of course, use our gifts and talents, but only if we first have a willing heart. As we are willing to be reshaped and remolded, and as we are willing to give the glory to God and not make ourselves to be God, then God can work through us. But without the desire to be supple on the potter's wheel, our efforts are merely human efforts. When our main belief is in ourselves, we are not able to bring the reality of God's presence to our churches.

Only God is able to do the miracle that is needed in our congregations. It is not up to us. Stop believing that God must go in your direction, and see what happens when you realize that God's ways are higher than your ways (Isaiah 55:8-9). As God looks over the earth seeking those who will be kingdom people, God looks at the heart. God seeks out those whose hearts are malleable, shapable, formable. God wants to make us in God's image so others can see the reflection of God's love in us. We are made to be mirrors—images that reflect back the one who creates and remakes us.

And that's what can happen for you. It might not be overnight, and it will probably take a lot of faith along the way, but you just might be surprised by what God has in mind for you and your church. Don't stop believing. Remember who is with you and step out and over the barrel that blocks your view. Remember your calling and be willing to watch God work in and through you and yours. Join in the fun, even when you don't know the answers or the way or the right thing. Give it a try!

You never know what God might do. You never know how God might realize the good news through your church!

FIVE

FAIL BIG AND FAST; GET UP AND DO IT AGAIN

reStore

Name your greatest failure. Does it pop into your mind quickly? I know my greatest personal failure, and I think I know my greatest failing as a pastor. My greatest failure as a person is that I turned away from God when I felt great pain. My first child died at four days of age. I had known God all my life, and in fact, could not remember a time without God. But when I stood before her little grave hole, I buried my faith. I don't even begin to understand why I did this, except I know great pain causes great pain. And so I walked away from God. For a year, I disbelieved in God.

But one day, I could deny God's presence no more. When Jim and I sat in a room together and a new little baby was placed in our arms,

I felt God's presence again. And I understood in that nanosecond that, while I had left God, God had never left me. I felt overwhelmed with repentance, and deeply loved by God, and now newly in love with my daughter.

My greatest failure became my deepest joy. Our children, Sara, Natalie, and Andrew, have continued to show me God's presence by their love. Every time I see them, I remember how God's Spirit whooshed over my broken heart with healing and great joy.

As a pastor, my greatest failure is cowardice. In the drive to succeed and fit in, I have been one of those pastors who have failed more times than not. Like Moses I have been afraid of using my voice; I have cowered behind the walls like Gideon; and I have hidden behind the baggage like Saul. But mostly, I have resisted further action because of cowardice, lack of faith, or a desire to fit in, to not make waves or rock any boats that might float by me. I know failure, and I know what it is to be a coward.

But I also know that failure has a silver lining. I know that when God uses us, our failures point to God and not to ourselves, and that is a beautiful silver lining. Though I occasionally bemoan my failures, God's love is fail-safe. God loves failure because it brings us to the place of relying on God alone.

Your church needs to risk failing more often. Your church needs to choose to fail big and fast and furiously. And then your church can understand the great joy in getting up and failing again.

This is not popular sentiment. But in times of change, we fail ourselves out of our current situations. We don't plan our way out; we fail our way out. The cultural idea of a turnaround company is to formulate the path to success, implement the plan, and tabulate the results. But God's way of change is to allow failure to reshape us. It is our skinned knees and our broken hearts that teach us the most. Imperfection, not perfection, is the way of growth.

Some people have learned this by acknowledging, even bragging, about their scars. "I got this line on my chest from heart surgery." Or, "These stretch marks are the result of giving birth to three beautiful children." We tell stories of failures when we recount how we made it through trials, because sometimes we realize that merely making it through is a remarkable event. When I ran the Marine Marathon, I was in the back of the pack the whole time. But those of us back there had a sense of pride: we were still running (well, sort of running). We were on the road, and though we were the last ones to cross the finish line, our failure was a great success. No one wrote us up in the papers, but we each still received a medal. Just for crossing the finish line.

Church, we need to fail more.

Some like to say it differently. They say, "Church, we need to risk more." It's not that I disagree with that statement, it's just that in order to risk we must first be willing to embrace, and get comfortable with, failure. Risking sounds wonderful until we realize it means falling flat on our faces a thousand times before we land on our feet.

To restore means,

1. to bring back into existence, use, or the like; reestablish: to restore order.

2. to bring back to a former, original, or normal condition, as a building, statue, or painting.

3. to bring back to a state of health, soundness, or vigor.

4. to put back to a former place, or to a former position, rank, etc.: *to restore the king to his throne.*

5. to give back; make return or restitution of (anything taken away or lost).[1]

59

When an old piece of furniture is restored, there is a risk taken. The risk is that the stripping will remove the well-known or beloved color or tint. Something is taken away, thus the risk, before the original beauty can be seen. Failure involves allowance for stripping down.

Where are your failures and what are they teaching you? What if instead of the denominational structures requiring us to report our successes, they asked us to count our failures? The real report card of advancement isn't the numbers of people who sit in our pews, but it is the number of souls who are transformed by the love of Jesus despite our failings.

Every failure brings potential for God to show up in glory. It is when we point to our own accomplishments that God keeps quiet, leaving us to brag about ourselves to walls that can't hear.

The whole story of our Scripture is human failings and God savings. Think of these losers: Adam and Eve, Abraham and Sarah, Moses, David, Solomon, Jonah, Job, Jeremiah, Peter, Paul, Mary Magdalene, and Martha. We know their shadow sides, but we also know they are examples of people who were greatly used by God.

It is only cowardice that prevents us from risking change and new life for the sake of the gospel of Jesus Christ.

Failure Comes with a Surprise

At CrossRoads United Methodist Church, we hosted a ministry called Prodigal's Home, led by Mike and Kim Ricker and associated with the Evangelical Lutheran Church. Prodigal's Home served homeless people, providing a breakfast and a weekly worship service. As they came on-site, we included them as one of our ministries. We served together, and we assisted in whatever way we could. We made it official that they were ours and we were theirs. But about five months into the process of working together, trouble showed up. Through a series of incidents, and a cease and desist order from the City of Phoenix, our lives changed. God took us on a journey of feeding the homeless, to standing with the homeless, and then, to fighting for the homeless. The journey gave us national attention, local significance, and internal searching to find out what it means to be the church. We would have never guessed or chosen this journey. But we were given a choice to follow God, and we chose that road. It has been a hard road. It is full of pain. And it is a delightful road. And it is full of joy. It is deeper, and broader, and larger than anything we could have planned for ourselves. That is what happens when we go God's way. We die to many things, and then we live to something new.

What we found out through this experience was that God wanted us to be about feeding. The church has forgotten how to do the basic thing of providing sustenance to the emptiness in our neighborhoods. And God will continue to call the church to feeding the people of our world. We start with feeding hungry bellies, and we end with feeding hungry souls. We are chefs, and it is our role to provide the communion that comes around food and being filled up. Jesus said in John, "Feed my sheep" (John 21:17).

He said it three times for emphasis. If my mama told me to do something three times, by the time she got to the third statement, I knew I'd better hurry and get it done! Jesus said it three times, and he said it as a part of his last words. Last words are important. They are synopsis statements that have great importance and value. We remember the last words of a loved one on the deathbed, and we never forget them. I remember my last conversation with my mother-in-law, and the thing she wanted to tell me was of the greatest importance for our past and the future. Jesus' last words on earth had great meaning. Jesus said simply, "Feed my lambs" (John 21:15).

61

Have you done that as a church? Are you in the feeding business? Whom are you feeding, and when are you feeding them? Do you know how many children are hungry in your town? How about in your neighborhood? How about across the street or next door?

Shortly after we began feeding and worshiping with the homeless, we got an e-mail from a city employee. A pastor-couple had come to her asking for food. She was told there were about one hundred children who were hungry and whose parents were out of work. They were unable to receive any funds or connect to programs with the city because most of these children were from undocumented parents, or were themselves undocumented. Our Arizona laws had cut them off from working, and now they were hungry—hungry and bold enough to march into the city offices and ask for help! The e-mail came to my box several times for a couple of weeks. Finally, with a spirit of a burdened pastor with too much to do, I answered the e-mail with a call. "What do you need?" The answer was, "Pastor Dottie, there are these children. They are hungry. Their parents can't work. The city can't help them. Can the church help?" I promised to pay a visit in the next few days. The truth is, I was exasperated by the load of work and the great many people who needed help.

But I got up from my desk right away, wanting to get it over with, and drove out to the address in north Phoenix. It was a trailer park. There was a set of three or four of them close together, and it was surrounded by a neighborhood of wealth. I knew this neighborhood, but I had never noticed this little pocket of poverty.

I knocked on the door of the trailer, but no one answered. So I wrote a note and left it on the back of my business card. Mike Ricker, the man who led Prodigal's Home in feeding and worshiping with the homeless, also went out later the same day. When he arrived, they were home, and he sat down and heard their story in broken English. He left with tears in his eyes, and he came to me and said, "Dottie, you've gotta meet these people! There are hungry children out there!"

We went out again. The pastor-couple had been praying for help. In fact, the husband had been fasting and praying for forty days. He said that in his prayer time God told him the answer to his prayers would be on his doorstep on the fortieth day. On the fortieth day, he found my card and note, and later, Mike Ricker knocked on his door. He asked Mike if he knew this person who left the card. We were, unknowingly, the instruments of an answered prayer for a group of about one hundred hungry children. Did God know it would take a couple of weeks to convince one tired, stubborn pastor to go out there to visit them? The thought makes my soul cry.

Out of that meeting, Prodigal's Home and CrossRoads United Methodist Church started providing food twice a week and supporting their ministry. One CrossRoads couple provided them with a car, since theirs had just gone to the car graveyard. The congregation provided the children with gifts at Christmastime and weekly support at their gatherings. We have walked hand in hand with them, and continue to do so, despite a political climate that is inhospitable to these lambs of God.

There are other hungers out there that need to be met. Start with the obvious and see what happens. Fall into your shortcomings, and be delighted in the ways God shows up!

BE CREATIVE

reForm

Creativity is required in reStart churches. It is essential. The creative church is one that is willing to be surprised, delighted, moved, changed, reconfigured, and, mostly, reformed. We may know about the Protestant Reformation, and the Wesleyan movement, but do we know what it takes to reform ourselves with the creativity of an artist?

Artists know something about reforming. They look at the world with different eyes. We pay high praise and, sometimes, large sums of money to see their perspectives on life. What if you saw your church as an artist would? Artists bring surprise renderings and views, unique shapes and forms, and topsy-turvy understandings. Artists move to destabilize, taking the form of confusion in order to bring a new light on a subject.

Today is the time for a reFormation of your local church.

65

Look at Your Setting with Young, Fresh Eyes

Be a missionary to your neighborhood.

You may know your neighborhood like the back of your hand. Sometimes what is familiar can become a stranger if we don't pay attention. When I first came to my current church, the people thought they represented the neighborhood, and that the neighborhood looked like they looked. The congregation was Anglo and elderly. They didn't know, or didn't see, that in the last few decades the neighborhood had changed and turned over. As young families grew up and children moved out, aging parents eventually moved to care homes or smaller houses. Now the neighborhood was filled with young families in old homes. Also, this church had never noticed the neighborhood to the north, which is Hispanic, poor, and young, with many refugees and homeless people. It was news to them that there was so much diversity around and that the community no longer looked like they did.

Usually it takes fresh eyes to know what is going on in the community. Those fresh eyes can be a new pastor, a visitor, or a consultant. Taking blinders off requires eyes that see, and sometimes we hesitate to see what will bring discomfort.

After understanding what is, one can begin to address the mission field that is around the corner.

Do Something Radical; Change Requires Change

Change requires change. I would even go so far as to say change requires radical change. That may seem obvious, but most of the time we approach change as if nothing needs to change. Churches say, "We want more young people in our community," while they continue to worship in a way that disconnects them from the generation they are seeking to reach. They wonder why the younger generations can't just learn the old hymns. While I do think hymns are great songs of the faith to learn, they must be approached differently if this generation is to hear them.

When a pastor is sent to a new church, often she or he is told to enact change and grow. The pastor is ready, even excited, to make needed changes. The new pastor takes the congregation at their word and begins to discuss the changes needed with the congregation. These are examples of the initial verbal responses:

> Pastor, we can't change the music. Our hymns are sacred.
>
> Take out the pews? If you do, I will leave this church and take my money elsewhere!
>
> The last pastor moved the cross to a different place, and I can't worship if the cross is not in the center of the altar. You are not going to move it, are you?

Responses like these reveal the congregation's hope that change requires no change. It is an illusion to tell ourselves that what is hoped for will happen as we do the same things we've been doing for decades. This kind of thinking smacks of illness of the mind and cowardice of the soul. Our Lord Jesus came to the earth and riled up the masses with such a radical message of love and purity that the religious bodies of his time were ready to kill him. And in the end, they did.

But the cowardice around change doesn't just lie with the followers who have been going to a particular church for a long time. The cowardice also resides in the hearts of the pastors and the denominational structure. Pastors are resistant to call for radical change because they know it means they will make many wonderful people upset, and they know the hierarchy is set for stability and not change. Their superintendents and bishops may not support change when the change brings letters of dissent to their desks.

Recently at a church council meeting, I shared with church leaders that I was writing this book, and that our church had been in this process for quite some time. I explained I would have led this change differently if I had been a more courageous leader when I first came to the church. One woman asked me what I would have done differently, since seven years later, it appears that we have become a new congregation. I admitted that if I had had more courage, and the assurance of a supportive denominational structure around the need for change, I would have asked to close down the congregation for a year, assisting those who were present to make a transition to other congregations nearby, of which there are many. After a year of helping the former parishioners make a change and allowing the property to remain unchurched, a new congregation could have been birthed on that site. The woman asked if that would have made this change easier or harder. I proposed it would have done both: made change harder and easier. It would have been a difficult and courageous move for those who had held the church together all these years. They would have lost much and would have been hurt deeply by the proposal that they go elsewhere. But it would have taken half the time to build a new congregation without the constraints of the former congregation fighting change with every little change that occurred. Energy could have been focused on reaching the community for Christ, rather than making people understand the reason change is needed, or worse, responding to complaints sent to the superintendent and the bishop.

Change is difficult even when it is understood as a necessary evil. Just a few weeks ago, at the beginning of worship, a woman bemoaned the fact that it is still hard for her to watch people enter the sanctuary with coffee and food in their hands. She said, "I know we need to do this and it reaches the community, but I still don't like it!"

I replied that it is hard, but God is remaking us and that's not easy.

And I let her know that I appreciated her patience with the changes and her prayers for the church she loves. She knew that the little changes mattered, and so she tolerated them, but not without internal unrest. This is the price of change. It costs something, and the greater the change, the greater the cost.

It is easy to point to the difficulty that the congregation experiences when they are challenged to make radical changes, but really, much of the hesitancy lies within the role of the pastor. Pastors are taught to go with the flow and not make waves. We are called peacemakers, and we don't like being labeled as troublemakers. We are schooled in the art of compromise at the same time we are schooled in the gospel of radical, costly love. Pastors find themselves in a tough spot: unsupported when they change even the little things. This atmosphere of nonsupport is the excuse we use not to change. Pastors recognize that it is a lonely walk forward. And some of us are concerned about putting bread on our own tables, and so we succumb to trivialities and dance around the language and the action of transformation. We keep transformation "out there" and "far away." It is our lack of courage and, some say, our lack of love for the lost that keep us stagnant, stable, and declining.

We need to be about more radical forms of change. Instead of discussing whether drinks can be in the sanctuary, or whether to get rid of the pews, we need to be imagining church in the future. We need to ask the basic questions for today:

Why do we have church?

Where do we have church?

When do we gather the church?

What are the forms of church?

How do we bring the gospel of Jesus Christ to this day and this people?

These are the questions we need to be struggling over together. Upon the answer to these questions lies the future of the church. Len Sweet says, "A journey to the center is a journey away from Jesus, who is found on the margins and in the edges and around the periphery. The cornerstone is not the center. To find and follow Jesus, we must decentralize our thinking and decenter everything."[1]

This is the day for radical decentering for the love of Jesus. If we love God and if we follow Jesus, we go where God goes. We follow the pillar of fire by night, and the cloud by day. When that takes us into the wilderness, we go. When we land on dry, desert terrain, there we remain. When we are called outside the doors of the church, we follow God there. When we lay down our understanding of leading the church, and transform ourselves into "Primary Followers,"[2] there we journey. Sweet reminds us that our call is not to be leaders but to be followers: "Jesus wasn't looking for leaders at all. Jesus was looking for followers."[3]

We've been doing a lot of leading lately, and we've skimped on doing the following. But during this radical time in history, it is following that is required. It is our time to follow God to the spaces, locations, and formations that Jesus dreams for us. And to do that, we must first consider the main questions.

Why Do We Have Church?

Why? is the basic question, and one that needs continual review. Why do church? Are we attending worship gatherings and church events because of mindless tradition, or are we steeped in the original tradition of making disciples of the world, including ourselves? Is church for socialization, or discipleship formation? Are we here to get along with the world, or are we here to transform the world? These things need to be considered.

Jesus spoke of the church twice. Once when he said: "I tell you that you are Peter. And I'll build my church on this rock. The gates of the underworld won't be able to stand against it. I'll give you the keys of the kingdom of heaven. Anything you fasten on earth will be fastened in heaven. Anything you loosen on earth will be loosened in heaven" (Matthew 16:18-19).

Jesus creates the church as something that will last even when we see it dying in its present form. The church is solid as a rock and able to set the course of history by its loosenings and fastenings.

The other scripture where Jesus speaks of the church is:

> But if they still won't pay attention, report it to the church. If they won't pay attention even to the church, treat them as you would a Gentile and tax collector. I assure you that whatever you fasten on earth will be fastened in heaven. And whatever you loosen on earth will be loosened in heaven. Again I assure you that if two of you agree on earth about anything you ask, then my Father who is in heaven will do it for you. For where two or three are gathered in my name, I'm there with them. (Matthew 18:17-20)

This scripture deals with correction when a brother or sister goes astray. It uses the church as a part of the process of restoring someone to unity and purity. But the interesting part of this passage is that it also mentions "loosening" and "fastening." It reminds the listener that when the body is gathered, there is the presence of God.

71

The two scriptures where Jesus mentions "church" both significantly mention this business of loosening and fastening. One is letting go of, and the other is holding on to. When we come together in the presence of God, the "why" of our gathering could just be to save the world through our loosenings and our fastenings.

So if the church is a body that is about these things, the question is: What are you loosening, and what are you fastening? When the church gets serious about its letting-go places and its holding-on places, then we will see the power of the gathered body in the world. Only then.

Where Do We Have Church?

The next question is: Where do we have church? We are used to having church inside a building that is "ours," and we are used to having church at the intersection of two particular cross streets in the community. Methodist tradition, the part of which we could be fastened to, took church outside to wherever the people gathered. Wesley went to the places where miners got off their shifts, and he became a field preacher instead of a pulpit preacher.[4] He came to love field preaching, and he was passionate about it, even though at first he resisted the idea of preaching beyond the walls of the church.[5] Instead of fastening ourselves to the idea of taking the gospel message to wherever the people gather, we have fought to keep everything just the same within the walls. But what if we had church in the natural gathering spaces: coffee shops, grocery store parking lots, mobile home parks, outside arenas before games, at the lakes, and in the parks? What are the local gathering places in your community, and how can you gather there?

When Do We Gather the Church?

The question of when to gather the body of Christ is similarly connected. We currently gather on Sunday morning and Wednesday evening, and some churches have branched out to Saturday evening. But we need to expand the times when people can attend a gathering of the sinners and the saints. Small groups are another aspect of church, currently rarely utilized because we fail to place the best lay leaders in charge of small groups or Wesleyan "classes." But these gatherings are central to faith development and they are the foundational method of discipleship-making for Wesleyans. Many more people would engage with the church if we expanded our understanding of when we meet.

CrossRoads has a small group called "Journey." They meet every other Friday night. But their location changes every time. They journey to a new hot spot in the community, a place where a certain musician will be heard, or they take a ride on the light rail together, stopping at a coffee shop to do the Bible study and Wesley accountability questions together. Every time they meet, they find a new location. The church can once again get creative around its location, and look at its property as a jumping board for raising money for the mission or as a jumping board to reach the community. The church property needs to be reimagined in its use, especially because many properties are sitting empty six days of the week, and on one day, they are still only half-full. Imagine the "where" of your church!

What Are the Forms of Church?

Another related question is: What are the forms of church? Today's church forms include the megachurch, minichurch, house church, multisite church, and so on. There are also urban churches, suburban and exurban churches, multiracial churches, and uniracial churches. Church has many forms. Emerging, missional, sacramental, and traditional are also common forms of church today. But surely our imaginations are not limited to the above listings! Wesley's form of church was nothing that he imagined, but rather it evolved as God called him forward to address the needs of a new frontier and a dwindling church. A revival swept across the lands as people gathered in small groups to grow disciples, do mercy, and attend to the disciplines of living a Christian life.

What about the possibilities of an occasional church (a church that meets once a month, and because of limited space, requires reservations); or a café church (where a free meal is provided, and one can pay if they want, or they can pay extra, or work for their food, and worship and deep discussion are incorporated into the mealtime); or a tailgate church (where services occur prior to sports events in arena parking lots, and food and drinks flow freely, as well as a lively interaction with the Wesley questions, much like truth or dare); or a recovery church (where persons working on being set free from addictions receive counsel, hope from preaching of the Word, and song, with commitments to live a healthy life); or a weight-loss church (where people band together to exercise, learn healthy eating habits, and fasten together to lean into Christ's love on the journey of health); or an artists' church (where artists, musicians, and drama are the media for the message of the Bible, and no preaching occurs in the standard way); or a mercy church (where people come together to feed the homeless, pack meals for starving populations, build homes for single mothers and their children, or perform other acts of mercy, and each gathering begins and ends with a short Bible study and proposed discussion topics to address while working side by side); or a job-search church (where people band together to share job leads and learn to keep up with connections, and end each time together with a half hour of deep prayer); or a silent church (where no word is spoken and no music is heard, in order to give space for peace and to listen to the voice of God).

You see that forms of church are endless, and yet we falter in our actions and in our risking forward because it is so very easy to do what we have been doing for so very long. We have become a lazy church. I don't think Jesus is pleased, and I know for sure the world is yawning at our ritualistic, lifeless gatherings.

How Do We Bring the Gospel of Jesus Christ to This Day and This People?

The last question to consider is: How do we bring the gospel of Jesus Christ to this day and this people? Some of the above forms also incorporate the answer to the "how" of church. But let's go deeper. If church is the gathering body that loosens and fastens, then how do we set people free and, at the same time, hold on tight to the central desire of loving Jesus?

SEVEN

FALL IN LOVE AGAIN

reAlign

Perhaps you've gone to a doctor who realigns your body through skeletal or energy adjustment. The visit comes about because of a pain in your back, and as the doctor starts working on you, he states that the actual source of your pain is not your back, but your jaw. When your jaw is misaligned, your head is not set straightforward. It has a tilt that leans one way or the other. In order for your pain to be relieved, you must first align the position of your head. So the doctor gently pulls, pushes, and touches your energy points with warm, healing hands. And before your back is even addressed, the pain goes away.

This is the same thing that happens when our love gets out of line. When the focus of the heart's desire is off-kilter, even slightly, the body pays for it with pain. Such is the groan of the church. While our hearts are warmed by the love of tradition or history, our focus has left our original love.

Our original love is that deep, unbreakable love we once felt for our Lord and Savior, Jesus the Christ. Gradually, we veered slightly to the left and began loving our works for Christ, or we veered slightly to the right and began loving our righteousness. But God didn't call us to love our works or our self-righteousness. God invited us to love God. God alone. And that invitation is not for a somewhat-love, but for a full-blown, all-out, once-in-a-lifetime kind of Great Love.

The haunting melody and tragic lyric of "Almost Lover," by A Fine Frenzy, reflects this tendency:

> Should have known you'd bring me heartache
> Almost lovers always do.

I wonder, as this melody plays through my soul, if the church we have created with our institutions and our rules and our lifeless gatherings is a church of an "almost love." I wonder if we tried to love, but failed. Truly the real church, the one imagined from the love of a risen Savior, is better at loving than we have been. Since our own children are turning away, and our closest relatives are not impressed with our non-witness, then surely we have to do some self-evaluation, and ask ourselves if we really did love well. Did we love Jesus, or just the idea of a good man on the earth? Did we have a passion, a heart strangely warmed, for the deep love of Christ? Did our faces shine as Moses' did when God spoke to us? Did we pray so that our knees ached when things got too hard? Or did we forget to attend to seeking God's face and God's voice? Did we get so comfortable with our status quo that we forgot to really love God, neighbor, and self? If we failed, I would say that is where our failure lies: in our choice to be an almost-lover with Jesus.

Revelation brings a similar message to the church at Ephesus. In a letter to the church, the writer proclaims:

I know your works, your labor, and your endurance. I also know that you don't put up with those who are evil. . . .

You have shown endurance and put up with a lot for my name's sake, and you haven't gotten tired. But I have this against you: you have let go of the love you had at first. So remember the high point from which you have fallen. Change your hearts and lives and do the things you did at first. (Revelation 2:2a, 3-5a)

The church at Ephesus was distracted by the goddess Diana and by cultural popularities. This church, originally founded by Paul with great passion, was now reeling from the consequences of focusing on a non-God entity.

Has the church as a whole gone through a major distraction process, so that over time, the whole body is misaligned? Perhaps the focus of the face of your church is pointed toward numbers, as in "butts in seats" and financial solvency. Or maybe your focus is on denominational and structural alignment, including paying 100 percent of expected giving and reporting great success in relation to stated vital signs. Or perhaps your focus is on feeding the hungry alone, or personal piety alone. If so, then as with the church at Ephesus, your tilted focus will be bringing you pain somewhere and sometime in the near future.

The interesting thing about bodily adjustments is that the doctor often works on the source of the problem, even though it might not be the place where we feel the pain. Just as a doctor might work on the jaw and the face in order to fix a back-pain problem, God chooses to go to the source of our struggles and heal that area. Otherwise, the pain will not fully subside and will return frequently. When your doctor says,

"Stand straight and don't lean on one hip," the instruction is to teach you how to realign your body for future health and wholeness.

When the church is crying out in pain, the thing to check is the love factor. How is our love for God? Does our passion for Jesus, the one who saved us, still burn bright? Do we still feel a great need for God? Love is the center, the lesson, the driver, the aligner. Love heals the pain.

The Corinthian church also went about learning this lesson. They were reminded that things like speaking beautifully, prophesying, knowledge of everything mysterious, and even faith were not of the same value as love. They were told that if they performed many acts of charity and mercy, they could brag about them, but their actions mattered little without the little thing called love. All those wonderful things will fail us, but love never fails. As we grow older, we understand the goodness of faith and hope. And even more so, we understand the foundation, the greatest gift, of love (1 Corinthians 13).

Jesus also focused us on loving God, neighbor, and self. The first love is for God. We wholeheartedly live out faithful love to God with our hearts burning bright with passion for God's way. And when that love comes into focus, we are able to love ourselves, and out of that love for the uniqueness that God created in each of us, we extend further love to our neighbors.

Some people make the mistake of thinking they can love God and neighbors without loving themselves. But that is wrong. No one can truly love his or her neighbor while hating or hurting themselves. This kingdom principle connects three loves: love for God, love for God's people, and love for God's person: yourself.

This is expressed by Marianne Williamson, who exposes this human thinking:

> You are a child of God. Your playing small does not serve the world. There's nothing enlightened about shrinking so that other people won't feel insecure around you. We are all meant to shine, as children do. We were born to make manifest the glory of God that is within us.[1]

Williamson expresses that the way of being a God-follower is not one in which the self is buried. Rather, the self is the instigator for loving the others in our lives.

Falling in love is tricky business. It happens instantly and is usually unexpected. But when it happens, it captivates our being. Our appetites fail us, our focus wanes in one area and becomes sharper for the loved one. The body, mind, and soul become attuned to the vibrations of the beloved.

Staying in love is a different animal. It takes determination, valuing, and faithfulness. To stay in love, one must attend to the other person even when the feelings have less pull or attraction. Staying in love means keeping one's eyes open and ears ready to see and hear the wants, needs, and desires that are beyond us. It takes searching for the beloved, even when the beloved is right before us.

And deep love requires the acceptance of forgiveness. Jesus showed the greatest act of forgiving love when, while nailed to the cross, he requested forgiveness for those who accused and killed him. He cried out to God in his greatest moment of pain: "Father, forgive them, for they don't know what they're doing" (Luke 23:34).

Following the example of Jesus is difficult. It requires that we forgive when we love. And it requires that we accept the forgiveness that is ours.

One of the greatest lessons of forgiveness came when I forgot a wedding. I was excited to marry Catie and Bren because I had walked the path with Catie for fifteen years. I first met her as a teen asleep on the church doorstep. She was cold, hungry, tired, and drug-addicted. Catie had a sweet smile that touched some chord inside, and I immediately liked her. Over the years, I came to love her as a beautiful, and yet tortured, child of God. I did everything I could to give her food and shelter, but Catie's drugs always trumped any assistance we provided. She kept coming back to talk and pray. When I would run across her in the street, I would stop, and Catie would run to me with her big smile and wrap her arms around me.

But I was helpless to help before the demon of addiction. This continued for fifteen years. I watched her go to the gates of hell and stay there. All I could do was pray as things turned from bad to worse to awful. One day I ran across Catie on the street, and she looked different. Her light was shining a little on the inside. She told me she had found a counselor who had helped her, and she had been in rehab. She actually went to rehab several times, and each time she came out a little freer. She got a job. She got off the street. Sometimes Catie would call me out of the blue just to tell me how well she was doing. I danced inside for Catie's transformation.

When she introduced me to her fiancé and asked me to perform their marriage ceremony, I was delighted. Her husband-to-be was a wonderful soul. He loved her well, and they were raising their daughter together. I was looking forward to this wedding more than most.

And I forgot it. It was on a Saturday, and I just plain forgot. I had no excuse for my inattention that day. I was in bed that night when the phone rang. It was Catie. "Dottie, I just want to know if you are okay." I jolted up out of bed, instantly realizing my mistake. I had forgotten Catie's wedding!

I apologized over and over on the phone, my spirit groaning for what had been lost by my inattention. "It's okay, Dottie. We just saw an accident on the way home, and we wanted to make sure that you were not in that accident. We are so glad you are okay." After we hung up, I was so distraught that I texted Catie, apologizing again. After a few words back and forth, Catie sent me this text:

> Dottie, after all the times I let you down over the years, this one mistake of yours doesn't begin to make up for the times you've forgiven me. I love you! Please don't feel bad.

Grace flooded my soul with Catie's words. I knew I had truly been forgiven. It is hard to describe the joy and release I felt. The experience of grace was so profound that something beautiful settled inside. I knew God's forgiveness was mine, even mine.

On Catie's wedding day, her father-in-law stepped up to "marry" them, operating from vows downloaded off the Internet. Catie said everything that could go wrong that day did go wrong. After the honeymoon, I went over to Catie and Bren's house and married them officially. As I walked into their home, I was overwhelmed by the thought *I'm walking into Catie's house!* Catie, my beloved young woman who had once stood on the precipice of death for years at a time, had a home! I had one other thought: *If they are mad at me, and give me the cold shoulder, I deserve it. Just buck up and take it.*

Her daughter greeted me with a big hug and a smile that echoed her mother's twinkling eyes. Everyone came around me, and we hugged and laughed and cried. I said "I'm sorry" again, and Catie said I must stop apologizing. She showed me pictures of her wedding. Catie looked like a beautiful princess in her wedding dress. The joy on her face was remarkable. As I looked at her photos, I couldn't help thinking about the first time I saw her, and how amazing that God saves us all by God's grace.

Catie and her handsome husband, Bren, sat by the fireplace, and I pulled up a footstool, and they quietly, tenderly, lovingly repeated their vows. They had eyes only for each other, and their love was a bright flame. After I pronounced them man and wife, we had more tears of joy, and laughter bubbled up again. It was truly the most beautiful marriage ceremony I'd ever been to. All because we all knew the power of forgiveness and the gift of grace.

In order for your church to love well, it must have forgiveness as its centerpiece. Forgiveness has been laid out on the Communion table and reaches out as a greeting in the narthex, in the words between those gathered, and is the covering for the memories of church meetings we'd like to forget. Forgiveness centers us in love.

How forgiving is your gathering of the body of Christ?

Disciplined Love

Our love for God also demands that we give that love due attention. The spiritual disciplines are called "disciplines" because they are not always easy to attend to. It takes time to stay in love with God. Certain habits can help, including the habit of reading scriptures, of starting the day out with thanksgiving prayers, of praying continually by directing our thoughts to God, and the habit of holding silence to hear God speak to us. These are some of the ways we attend to loving God and staying in tune with the Divine.

The discipline of love requires that we pray for one another. Jesus prayed for his disciples this way:

> "I'm praying for them. I'm not praying for the world but for those you gave me, because they are yours. Everything that is mine is yours and everything that is yours is mine; I have been glorified in them. I'm no longer in the world, but they are in the world, even as I'm coming to you. Holy Father, watch over them in your name, the name you gave me, that they will be one just as we are one. When I was with them, I watched over them in your name, the name you gave to me, and I kept them safe. None of them were lost, except the one who was destined for destruction, so that scripture would be fulfilled. Now I'm coming to you and I say these things while I'm in the world so that they can share completely in my joy." (John 17:9-13)

Jesus' love and care for his disciples was obvious. He was crying out for their protection during and after his trial of death. He would not leave them alone.

A loving church prays for one another. A loving church prays together in church. A loving church kneels at altars and sings worship songs as an act of prayer. As we lift our souls to God in wonder, we also lift one another up, asking God for strength to make it through the days of our living and courage to love the world well.

We have choices. Love or almost-love. Adele sings a song called "Rolling in the Deep." It says,

There's a fire starting in my heart,
Reaching a fever pitch and it's bringing me out the dark.

The fire that burns within our hearts-strangely-warmed by God's love is still present. You may feel only an ember at this moment, but with an ember and the wind of the Holy Spirit, a flame can spark that turns into a roaring fire. God's love is burning within us. We can let it out or we can smother it. The choice is ours.

Our decision can be to face God, realign the body of Christ in love, and set our souls on fire. For when we sow love, it is love that will be reaped. Let the love begin.

EIGHT

GO DEEP
WITH GOD

reLease

Releasing is the hardest thing. It calls for letting go of our own desires and focusing on God alone. To release is:

To withdraw, revoke, also to liberate.

To relinquish, quit, let go, leave behind

To relax

To surrender[1]

Releasing is letting go again, liberating again, relaxing again, and surrendering again. Releasing to God is the ultimate act of trust. Releasing brings a new lease on life.

We learn about releasing when a child goes to school for the first time, then again when he walks out the front door of your home and into his own experience of adulthood. We release when we submit to anesthesia, and then surgery, trusting that the doctor knows what she claims to know. Running to the bathroom is about release. We release when we walk away from a difficult marriage or an abusive relationship. Release happens when we say good-bye to our mother and give her over to the eternity of heaven. Release happens frequently. We know this phenomenon. But that doesn't mean we like it. It does not come naturally to us.

But we must do this even if it is in no way easy. You see, the world is hungry for God. The words of Matisyahu in "King Without a Crown" sum it up:

> Wanta be close to you, yes I'm so hungry.
> . . . .
> I give myself to you from the essence of my being.

Because the world is hungering and thirsting after God, we release our own understandings and work alongside God's way. We set down our way and pick up God's way of living. We set free the things that bind us to this earthly fastening, and we loosen the kingdom way. We give ourselves to God from the essence of our being.

As a pastor to churches on the precipice of death, I have looked everywhere for the answers to our question: How do we live again? Even though death and resurrection are our central story, we have little experience in risings. We especially lack experience in one of the most difficult of all risings: church risings. So I attended many conferences that taught me how to pay attention to the mechanics of church. Workshops focused on the "how-to's": "How to Grow a Church"; "How to Grow a Children's Program"; "How to Add Technology in Worship";

"How to Develop Small Groups." While much was gleaned in attending these national conferences, there was a little nudging within that questioned every methodology and formulation. The nudging was about the question: Is this all we are about, Church?

What I really longed for, where my hunger lay, was in the desire to draw near to God. As a person who was up front during weekly worship, at these conferences I wanted to be in the back row, unknown and unwatched, so that I could worship with abandon. I wanted to worship with other pastors and churchgoers so that our voices of praise could touch the face of God. I wanted to feel the rush of the Holy Spirit fill the room through the preaching, the singing, and the abandon. That's what I wanted to conference around. I just wanted to kneel and pray together, asking God, to guide us instead of church leaders.

I am a workshop leader and conference speaker myself, so I say this with all due respect and honor to those who prepare the best they can to address church topics. I love presenting because I love preaching, and I feel God's presence in that moment. But I have often wondered how these gatherings would be different if we just gathered to worship God, pray for one another and our churches, and seek God's face.

I wonder if we would come home empty of informational notebooks, and yet filled in our souls. That is what we really long for. We long for God. We long to see, touch, smell, and feel God's presence and amazing love. We long to go deep with God. Pastors and churchgoers really just want to gather across the globe and be touched by the greatest amazing grace. Somehow the sense that this movement of the Spirit is what is needed is rising. And at the same time it is being ignored. We continue to go to conferences to learn, as if our brains can do what the Spirit is calling for. Intelligence and managerial expertise will always reach a place of limitation. But with God's Spirit our spirits can soar limitlessly.

That's where our deepest hunger lies.

To go deep with God is like diving into the pool. When we are still worried about our lack of experience and ability to swim, we jump in feetfirst. Somehow that comforts us because we are in our natural position. And it seems as though we can swim to the edge better when we don't have to move our body into the upright position. Feetfirst jumping is all about control.

But when we know that the water will support us and that its fluidity will make it easy to move in any direction, then we gain trust. When we don't feel the need to control the circumstances, we can dive in headfirst. The water breaks with the first touch of the finger to the water, and the body glides with both speed and grace. And truly, we swim to the edge much quicker. Diving in headfirst takes trust.

Most of us Christians are feetfirst jumpers. (Some are even more hesitant, and wade in inch by inch.) We want to maintain a semblance of control as we follow God. We want the option to do things the way we have been doing them all our lives. We want the known factor, because then we feel more control over the outcome.

But divers are free to swim with abandon. Divers know the process of giving in to God so well they end up experiencing the greatest joy. Divers know God more fully. They trust God with everything they have inside them. Divers go deep, touch the depth of God's love, and surface with joy in experiencing the deep waters.

I Can Only Imagine the Love

Recently we got the call that my mother-in-law, Mimi, was about to pass into eternity. Our family flew out to be with her and say our good-byes. The Frank family loves to sing together, and it is something they have been doing as long as they can remember. When the whole family had arrived, we began singing to Mimi. Her children and grand-children gathered around her bed and sang all the old hymns. She sang along when she could, and you could see her face glowing through the singing.

At one point they sang Mercy Me's "I Can Only Imagine." The words of wonder moved us to the depth of our souls. Soon our beloved was going to meet Jesus, and the song attempts to express what that moment might be like. As you stand in God's glory, will you dance or be still? Will you stand or fall? Will you shout or even be able to speak?

With tears all around, we sang about the moment when Mimi would meet Jesus.

Our imaginations are inadequate to the true experience of God's love. When we see God face-to-face, it will be inexpressible. To be in God's presence is the greatest joy in life. It takes being willing to dive in headfirst and go deep in our love. It takes giving up our need to control our lives and our churches.

Imagine the church you are a part of being able to stand before Jesus. What would your response be? Would you be weeping for joy or for regret? Would your congregation dance together, or would you fall on your faces, weeping before God? Would you be able to point to the fruit of lives, including your own, that reflect Jesus, or would your "glory" be past and external?

I think Jesus wants to make a visit to your church so that your imaginings can become real and your transformation deep.

Jesus' disciples could imagine this transformation because they lived through it. They spent their days with Jesus up to the end. They watched him pray with blood-tears in the garden of Gethsemane; they saw him arrested and taken away; they heard the lies told about him at his trial and they saw him carry the cross through the streets; and finally they saw him as he laid his life down on the cross, receiving the pain of the world on his body. They knew when the women reported his death. They were there.

For a while they hid out, but things were happening fast. The women were saying that he had risen and they were seeing strange things. When the disciples went to confirm the women's words, they saw the tomb was empty. And then Jesus started appearing to them! This was beyond anything they'd ever imagined before! The one they loved and grieved was up and walking around in their midst.

Finally, they had a face-to-face meeting, where they ate together, and Jesus invited them to touch his body, just to confirm that he was real and not a figment of their imagination. And Jesus opened their minds to see the Scriptures in a new way. He told them,

> "This is what is written: the Christ will suffer and rise from the dead on the third day, and a change of heart and life for the forgiveness of sins must be preached in his name to all nations, beginning from Jerusalem. You are witnesses of these things. Look, I'm sending to you what my Father promised, but you are to stay in the city until you have been furnished with heavenly power." (Luke 24:46-49)

When Jesus rose from the dead, he did it so that we could have a change of heart and life, and so that we could preach the forgiveness of sins. Jesus didn't go through all that suffering so that we could be about the same ol', same ol'. Jesus wanted us to be forgiven and transformed in our living.

Our churches are not about the numbers of people we count every year and report to the denominational structures. Our churches are not about the cool things we do that we like to brag about. Our churches are not about having a place to belong. The gathering of people is for the purpose of forgiveness and transformation.

The Wesleyan method of creating avenues of forgiveness and transformation was the class meeting. This small gathering of Christians met weekly to hold one another close as they walked the path of followership together. They read Scripture, shared concerns and trials, confessed their sins, and explained the places where they were involved in acts of mercy. They wanted to hear, "How goes it with your soul?" They made a list of questions so that they didn't get off-topic.[2]

Today, many churches have small groups for Bible study, but they do not always make the leap of holding one another accountable to faithfulness and fruitfulness. They have the form of Methodism, but not the heart of being a Methodist. The heart of being a Methodist is to want your heart to burn, or at the very least, to be strangely warmed by the moving presence of the Holy Spirit.[3]

We have lost the desire to go deep with God, especially when doing so requires discipline and meeting together regularly. But Jesus' example is one of meeting every day, walking around the country to give the gospel to many. And he walked this journey with his disciples until, finally, they ended up with him at the end of his life.

Jesus then took this little band of "first followers"[4] to a place near Bethany, and after giving them a blessing, he rose up to the heavens to be face-to-face with his Father. After thirty-some years of seeing God's face darkly, as through a dimly lit mirror, Jesus now could be fully present with God! And when Jesus rose to the heavens, the disciples saw it, and their response was to worship! I can imagine they laughed and cried and sang and danced and let out whoops of joy! Can't you see them jumping up and down, and falling on the ground, rolling in the grass with laughter and tears? The Bible says that after this worship party, they went back home to Jerusalem, and they were "overwhelmed with joy. And they were continuously in the temple praising God" (Luke 24:52-53).

When you know where your loved one is going, and the love you have, it causes you to be overwhelmed with joy.

I saw it happen when Mimi passed on to the other side of glory. After the whole family sang to her, Mimi rallied for weeks. But then we got another call: "Mimi is going now." The children and their spouses came out. We stayed around her bed during her last breaths, and finally, Mimi stopped struggling to breathe and let go of her earthly burdens. At 3:03 on a Sunday afternoon, Mimi went to Big Church to be with Jesus. The response in the room was one of joy! We felt her joy of release, and truly everyone was so happy for her. We were sad too. We will miss her physical presence, her smile, and the sparkle in her eyes. But tears were mixed with beautiful expressions of joy. Our beloved was seeing Jesus face-to-face for the first time, and we could imagine her giggle of delight, her eyes brighter than bright, and her feet jumping for joy! She made it to the other side. No more sorrow. No more pain. Only fully present to God.

Jesus came so that we can be transformed and forgiven, and this transformation is about seeing God's face as much as possible on this side. On this side of eternity, we can trust in God so deeply that we allow the beauty on the inside to trump any beauty on the outside. We seek those things that are like God: the fruit of allowing God to forgive us, to remake us, and to restart our witness.

We are in dire need of deep churches. We have plenty of surface churches. But we need churches that are willing to suffer along with Christ so that the world can see God. We need churches that are able to ignore the markers of worldly success and dive into the makings of being last, being servants, being changed.

Does your neighborhood and your city see the witness of your church as one that makes a difference, or do they see you as a stable location at the intersection of your cross streets, a place that has historical remembrances but makes no major difference in the city? Do they know you as deep, or as shallow? Are you willing to be forgiven, and then are you willing to be changed in the depths of your souls?

In order to go deep with God we must learn the true joy of full surrender. *Surrender* is not a popular word in our society today, but it is what takes us deep. Are you ready to surrender your idea of church to God? Are you ready to allow God to trump all of your efforts, giving in to the path that is unfamiliar yet filled with the light of Christ?

ReStart churches choose to go deep by fully reLeasing to God.

STICK
WITH IT

reInvigorate

Half the battle is staying the course. In order to stay the course, your church must experience invigoration constantly. Without reinvigoration, stagnation sets in, and you begin looking for anything new to give your church a boost. When you search for the new thing with desperation, you are in the danger zone. You are in danger of blowing with the winds of deceit, of being easily swayed by ideas that may take you off the course God has set. Once you know what God is up to in your church, half the battle is staying focused on that path.

Mary, the mother of Jesus, knew something about staying faithful to the course set for her by the heavenly arena. She was just a young girl when the angel gave her the message:

"Rejoice, favored one! The Lord is with you!" She was confused by these words and wondered what kind of greeting this might be. The angel said, "Don't be afraid, Mary. God is honoring you. Look! You will conceive and give birth to a son, and you will name him Jesus. He will be great and he will be called the Son of the Most High. The Lord God will give him the throne of David his father. He will rule over Jacob's house forever, and there will be no end to his kingdom." (Luke 1:28b-33)

Notice the detail that the angel provided for Mary. Not only would she give birth to a son, she was told his name, and his connection to God, and his connection to King David, and that his life would be so influential that his kingdom would last forever. This is no ordinary child. Mary needed to hear the detail of her child's importance so that she could hang on to it when things got tough.

The response of the world was sent to stamp the importance of Jesus' birth on Mary's heart. Elizabeth responded when she saw that Mary was pregnant. A response came in the form of angels singing in the heavens and shepherds coming to worship him. Another response came from wise kings, traveling from afar, bringing gifts of frankincense, gold, and myrrh. The world responded to the glory of the baby Jesus when Simeon held Jesus, knowing that now he had seen his salvation, and he could die in peace. And the world responded when Anna prophesied to the crowd that this child was the redemption of Jerusalem. Mary noted all of these events, and she tucked their significance deep in her heart.

So Mary had something to hang on to when life got tough. When her twelve-year-old son lingered behind, conversing with the teachers in the temple, Mary remembered his eternal role. When she heard that people were healed when Jesus prayed for them, Mary remembered whose he was. When she saw how the crowds gathered wherever he went, and how they held on to every word that came out of his mouth, Mary recalled the shepherds' praise and their description of the angelic choir in the sky. When Jesus was arrested, Mary remembered Simeon's and Anna's words with an ache in her belly. When he hung on the cross, Mary recalled the promise that his kingdom would have no end. And when she received the body of her dead son for burial, Mary remembered that he was the Son of the Most High.

Mary held on to the promises and the focus of her child's life, because without those promises she would have been lost, confused, and distraught. Mary found her peace throughout her son's life, even the peace that passes all understanding, because she had been told again and again who her son really was. Mary remained faithful to the end.

Thinking of Mary's faithfulness puts our situations in a different light. How can we be faithful to God and not the world's idea of the church? Some part of your setting needs to stay the course. The knowledge of what needs holding fast will come when you recall God's call for your church. Eugene Peterson states: "Religion in our time has been captured by the tourist mind-set."[1]

A tourist merely visits a location, taking pictures, getting an overview, and seeing sites from a distant viewpoint. A tourist thinks it might be great to live in the locale, but is not ready to change addresses in order to know the life of the town he or she is visiting. A tourist Christian is one who is merely ogling the lifestyle without developing a relationship with the town mayor and with the townspeople. Tourist Christianity is unwilling to suffer, sacrifice, or remain faithful. Tourist Christians like the idea of being a follower of Christ, but they are not willing to pay the price. Peterson comments on Friedrich Nietzsche's idea of a long obedience, stating: "It is this 'long obedience in the same direction' which the mood of the world does so much to discourage."[2]

Our instant mind-set leaves little room to provide space for intentional reflection. The place for determined discipleship is the foundation of deepening our faith.

CrossRoads has a history of feeding people, worshiping with creativity, and caring for children and families. But when I first arrived on the church step, the only one of these things still in place was feeding the homeless. There were very few children and young families, and the worship style was traditional without creativity. (Traditional worship can be creative and historical at the same time, but many times it is more rote than real.) So we immediately began a new service to reach the families, children, and all the rest of the neighbors. It had a contemporary flare, with a mix of gospel, rock, and Latin beats.

Those who were there already wondered why we were starting something new when our current service was not full. Since we proved every Sunday that this service was not reaching out, it was time to go a new way. At the same time, we stayed the course of a traditional service for the elderly, because they needed to worship God in the way that made sense to their spirits as well.

At first we had only ten people in the new service! And then we grew to thirty people. We stayed between ten and thirty people for a long time—maybe even a year. Then we bumped up to sixty people, and we hovered at that number for quite some time. Currently, we worship with about seventy to ninety people. The service is filled with children. It is filled with people who fall along the full spectrum between homelessness and wealth. We are made up of Anglos, Hispanics, African Americans, and persons of mixed heritage. The worship is lively and heartfelt. It is a vibrant community of faith that is growing closer to God every week. We are in no way close to full, nor are we close to perfect. But we remain faithful.

The interesting side effect is that the traditional service is still hanging on. My personal thought was that this service would eventually die out as the elderly faithful ones entered into eternity. But God had other plans. We have lost many people to death. And the amazing thing is that more elderly, mixed with some young faces, have started coming to that service as well. Just when I thought it was getting too small to continue, we had a little growth spurt that has continued. God remained faithful to us even when we were filled with doubts.

That's the way it works with God. God is faithful whether or not we are faithful. Our response to the overwhelming faithfulness of God is to be faithful in return. Sometimes that means staying the course when others think that thirty people are not worth the time and the effort. Sometimes it means remembering the original call and reach of your church and implementing your genuine call, letting go of the calls that distract you. Sometimes being faithful to God means being true to the development of disciples of Jesus Christ, even when that comes at the expense of numerical and statistical significance for your denomination.

Jesus stayed the course with twelve men and some women. He poured his life into theirs. He taught them life-changing ideas, and he walked with them every day. They became part of his healing touch, they ministered to the crowds with him, they experienced the miracles on the land and the sea, and they heard his words every day. Jesus went small and centered in order that the whole world could know God. Sometimes we get persuaded that growing a church is about being faithful to numbers. But the gospel truth is, growing a church is about being faithful to following God with a few people, and then watching God do what God will do in our midst.

According to theologian Robert E. Webber, the earliest form of evangelism was considered a process in which one was involved in a community of faith, which eventually led to the decision of baptism. The steps of conversion in Hippolytus's *The Apostolic Tradition*, Webber says, looked like this:

1. a time for Christian inquiry, known as the *seeker* period;

2. a time of instruction, when the converting person was known as a *hearer*;

3. an intense spiritual preparation for baptism, when the candidate was known as a *kneeler*; and

4. a time after baptism for incorporating the new Christian into the full life of the church, when the newly baptized person was known as *faithful*.[3]

The development of a new Christian was taken seriously, attended to in a plodding fashion, and accounted for in community. Faithfulness was taught even in the beginning stages of faith development.

Compare and contrast this to today's setting. Many churches have classes for new members. These classes are usually a onetime event lasting a couple of hours. The class offers information about the church, but says nothing about the deeper life of discipleship. The classes are taken as a way to check something off a list. There is no time for Bible study, service in the community, or faith development through addressing the Wesley questions over a period of time.

Pastor Mark Batterson describes the attendance to the work of following Christ when he was learning to preach. When he was first called to preach, he decided to preach at every opportunity he could get. So he began preaching at local nursing homes and homeless shelters. He had a circuit of nursing homes that he covered regularly. Batterson says, "I was the John Wesley of the nursing-home circuit."[4]

He said it wasn't a glamorous post, and many people were inattentive or even rude. But it mattered to a few souls, and it matured his preaching style. What circuit are you willing to work in order to learn how to be a disciple of Jesus Christ? Many Christ-followers feel comfortable attending worship services on Sunday, but are uncomfortable stepping out in hosting a discipleship group, or attending to the social justice requests that come from the church's missions team. We are all called to make disciples of Jesus Christ, yet we hesitate to even ask our friends and neighbors to come with us to worship God, embarrassed by the fact that we are people of faith. But what if we had a plan to be invitational daily? What if we developed a circuit and stayed faithful to it? We just might see the power of God moving in our midst if we took that one step forward.

To reinvigorate means to "give new life or energy to."[5] It is synonymous with "freshen, refresh, renew."[6] Everything old needs some refreshing and new energy. If you have a beautiful piece of antique furniture, it will likely need repair and a new coat of varnish in order to bring back its original functionality and beauty. And so the church. Old ways can be beautiful and old traditions can be functional, but they need continual renewal.

John Wesley writes about the distinguishing traits of a Methodist in "The Character of a Methodist."[7] These foundational characteristics focus on remaining faithful to our tradition in Jesus Christ:

1. A Methodist is one who has "the love of God shed abroad in his heart by the Holy Ghost given unto him"; one who "loves the Lord his God with all his heart, and with all his soul, and with all his mind, and with all his strength."

2. He is therefore happy in God, yea, always happy, as having in him "a well of water springing up into everlasting life," and overflowing his soul with peace and joy.

"Perfect love" having now "cast out fear," he "rejoices evermore."

3. And he who hath this hope, thus "full of immortality, in everything giveth thanks"; as knowing that this (whatsoever it is) "is the will of God in Christ Jesus concerning him."

4. For indeed he "prays without ceasing."

5. And while he thus always exercises his love to God, by praying without ceasing, rejoicing evermore, and in everything giving thanks, this commandment is written in his heart, "That he who loveth God love his brother also."

6. For he is pure in heart.

7. Agreeable to this his one desire, is the one design of his life, namely, "not to do his own will but the will of Him that sent him."

8. For as he loves God, so he keeps his commandments; not only some, or most of them, but all, from the least to the greatest.

9. For his obedience is in proportion to his love, the source from whence it flows.

10. By consequence, whatsoever he doeth, it is all to the glory of God.

11. Nor do the customs of the world at all hinder his "running the race that is set before him."

12. Lastly, as he has time, he "does good unto all men"; unto neighbours and strangers, friends and enemies.[8]

These marks of a Methodist help us remain faithful to God in the middle of living life's pressures. They especially give us focus when society invites otherwise. In order to stay the course, we must be faithful to the tradition of continual renewal. God transforms us always:

Look! I'm doing a new thing;
>   now it sprouts up;
>   don't you recognize it?
>   I'm making a way in the desert,
>   paths in the wilderness. (Isaiah 43:19)

Staying the course with God means being willing to be refreshed in our traditions and being true to the original call of our particular church.

TEN

CHOOSE JESUS
OVER "SUCCESS"

reBirth

In her book, *Salvation on the Small Screen?,* Nadia Bolz-Weber addresses the contrast between Christianity as seen on the television screen and the genuine simple faith of Christ-followers.[1] She decides to watch twenty-four hours of Christian television on Trinity Broadcasting Network, inviting friends and theologians in to take shifts watching with her. With each show, she counts the total dollar amount of requests for funds, number of scriptures used, total cost of products advertised for sale, doctrinal emphasis, and number of times Jesus is mentioned.[2] The interesting thing was that "Jesus" was mentioned rarely in each show, with some never mentioning Jesus.[3] If the evangelical branch of Christianity, as it is seen on television, is lacking in focus on Jesus Christ, then perhaps there is evidence we are losing our center. Our heart warmed for Christ is growing cold when we forget who our Savior is.

In the church we have been sold a bill of goods for so long that we not only believe it, we have started proselytizing it. The line goes like this:

The church is successful if we gather large bodies of people together at one time, putting on conferences to tell others how to do the same, and build big buildings to house these crowds.

A successful church has no money problems, pays all its apportionments, has debt sufficient to show growth, and is led by a pastor who excels at fund-raising.

The successful church is uniform. It gathers people of like economic status, similar races and cultures, and close age categories.

The successful church employs staff to handle all essential functions, and is, therefore, a staff-led community.

The success of a church's mission is seen by sending money "over there" and by sending short-term mission teams to other places.

The successful church is pastor-centered. It is led by a dynamic, charismatic, CEO pastor who draws a crowd because of his (not her) personality.

The successful church is consumer-oriented. It takes care of the congregation in the same way consumers are given preferential treatment.

These are some of the messages that churches pass on, with or without intention. Some Christians take pride in their church based on these categories, bragging about which church they are connected to, and how many people attend along with them.

But is this really God's idea of a "successful" church? A church centered on Jesus takes his message seriously and lives life in a manner that is counterintuitive to our current understanding of "success." The Jesus church focuses on these things:

> "You must love the Lord your God with all your heart, with all your being, with all your strength, and with all your mind, and love your neighbor as yourself." (Luke 10:27)

> So those who are last will be first. And those who are first will be last. (Matthew 20:16)

> "Be careful that you don't practice your religion in front of people to draw their attention. If you do, you will have no reward from your Father who is in heaven." (Matthew 6:1)

> Jesus said to everyone, "All who want to come after me must say no to themselves, take up their cross daily, and follow me. All who want to save their lives will lose them. But all who lose their lives because of me will save them." (Luke 9:23-24)

> "But the time is coming—and is here!—when true worshippers will worship in spirit and truth." (John 4:23)

"How can you believe when you receive praise from each other but don't seek the praise that comes from the only God?" (John 5:44)

"You are truly my disciples if you remain faithful to my teaching. Then you will know the truth, and the truth will set you free." (John 8:31-32)

The pattern of scriptural messages from Jesus does not paint a picture of "success." To be a follower of Jesus Christ is costly. It requires sacrifice, giving up what comes naturally to us: seeking ourselves. It calls for us to seek God first, and to leave ourselves behind. It calls for all the glory to be for God, and not for ourselves.

When I was a child, I attended my father's congregation in Mexico on Sunday afternoons. Every week there was a time of witness, and people would stand up and tell something that had been happening to them and how God had met them during their time of joy, difficulty, family problem, and so on. At the end of every witness they would say, "Por el honor y gloria de Dios!" Translated, this means, "For the honor and glory of God." It was their humble way of acknowledging that everything in their lives was to honor God. When they were hungry and had to put the kids to bed for days so they wouldn't use up too much energy, it was *for the honor and glory of God.* When they found a new job and now they would have food on the table, it was *for the honor and glory of God.* When they sang a song off-key and with gusto and feeling, it was *for the honor and glory of God.* When they just wanted to thank God that they could make it to worship this week, it was *for the honor and glory of God.* This phrase filled their souls and bubbled over into their lives so that they truly understood that living the life of a

110

Christian was not living for themselves, but so that God's glory could manifest itself on earth through them.

And yet our current church has the tendency to take the spotlight away from God and point it at our church, our pastor, and our position in the community. We frequently forget that all we are to do is to honor the one who saved us from ourselves, from the evil, and from the alternate way of living.

The life of a Christ-follower is not easy. It takes decision, commitment, and the understanding that love has a steep learning curve. Learning to love is the same as learning to lean. Leaning into God in Christ Jesus will stretch us more than anything we have previously known. The stretching will hurt and will be uncomfortable. But it will be so that God will do more work in and through us than we could do ourselves.

But God must wonder if we really do love God when viewing our churches. Perhaps God thinks of us in a similar fashion as Adele does of a lost lover when she sings in her song "I Can't Make You Love Me."

> Don't patronize, don't patronize
> 'Cause I can't make you love me if you don't.

When God looks at our churches, does God feel the love? Does God feel patronized? Or does God feel the loss of a love gone bad?

We all know the experience of a grand love that has lost its fervor. Time, difficulties, and life transitions can steal what was once beautiful, strong, and good. We experience this on a human level, and we also know this can happen with our love for God. We even admit that there are times when we don't feel so close to God, when we wonder where God went. This happens when we focus on things other than Jesus. This happens when our idea of "successful church" trumps our idea of "follower of Christ." It takes only a slight deviation for the whole body to get out of alignment with our Great Love.

What we need is a good, old-fashioned rebirth.

The story of Ezekiel and the valley of dry bones is significant for our time. Remember the story: Ezekiel is led out by the Spirit of God to view the valley, which is filled with dead, extremely dry bones. God asks him if the bones will be able to live again. Ezekiel must've thought, *Well, God, not really!* but instead he said, "LORD God, only you know" (Ezekiel 37:3).

God told him to speak to the bones and to say,

> "Dry bones, hear the LORD's word! The LORD God proclaims to these bones: I am about to put breath in you, and you will live again. I will put sinews on you, place flesh on you, and cover you with skin. When I put breath in you, and you come to life, you will know that I am the LORD." (Ezekiel 37:4b-6)

It's amazing that when God is going to do something in our midst, God first gives a warning call. Ezekiel first prophesied that something different was coming in the near future. He prepared the bones for the great transformation that was theirs.

When he spoke this warning call to the bones, there was a great response of noise and quakes. The bones came together, and they had sinews and flesh and skin. But they still had no breath.

The turmoil we are currently experiencing in the church is the earthmoving and noisemaking quake of a church about to be changed. It causes us on the local church level to cry out in pain and agony over the change. It is an earthmoving and stained-glass-shattering transformation. Just knowing what we will lose and what we will have to let go of in order to be reBorn is enough to make us lose our sanity.

But even in this great transition there is hope. We see the signs of new sinews, new flesh, and new skin on the edges of Christianity. Formations of groups of dedicated followers of Jesus are making a difference, and their presence is being felt. We are beginning to question all that we have assumed, and we are taking another look at what matters and what just no longer makes sense. We've been rattled to the bone, and the shaking did us so much good.

But even though the dry bones now had flesh, skin, and sinew on them, they did not have breath in them. And so Ezekiel was told to speak the future into the present and to proclaim that the winds from the four corners of the earth would come into these bones and bring them breath. As he spoke, the bones breathed, and when they breathed, they stood up on their feet. Suddenly you could see that this former heap of dead, dry bones was now a very large company of people.

As God moves in us, the body of Jesus Christ, which forms itself around a local church, it is the breath of the Holy Spirit that will fill us and empower us for the work of the company of saints. The Wesleyan movement was bent and shaped by the movement of the Spirit of God in the middle of ordinary people in England and in America. There was weeping, and heartfelt repentance, and there was dancing, and there were spirit-words being proclaimed out of the mouths of ordinary women and men. Yet when a stranger enters our places of worship, they see only the appearance of dead dry bones and quiet, barely-singing-and-not-even-worshiping skeletons. But this is our past and not our future. Our future hope is that the winds of God's Spirit will fill us again and give us a chance at the Great Do-Over. This is the only way our churches will be remade: by a movement of the Holy Spirit.

But God wasn't done with these dead, dry bones yet! God spoke to Ezekiel again and said,

113

"'I'm opening your graves! I will raise you up from your graves, my people, and I will bring you to Israel's fertile land. You will know that I am the LORD, when I open your graves and raise you up from your graves, my people. I will put my breath in you, and you will live. I will plant you on your fertile land, and you will know that I am the LORD. I've spoken, and I will do it.' This is what the LORD says." (Ezekiel 37:12-14)

This time, God is going to the very graveyards and setting them free of the dead places. God doesn't stop at restarting churches. God continues to the grave and restarts what has already been buried. God conquers even death.

Every local church has places that are so dead, they are buried-dead. These places stink, rot, and are swarming with varmints. They are dry, lifeless, unmoving bones lying in a dry and desolate desert. Even the most stubborn of us, those who fight change the most, can see the places where we are so dead that we experience the hopelessness of being underground. But God intends to visit your graveyards. And God intends to make something out of these dead places. And God intends to bring resurrection to your deadest-of-dead settings.

And really, all we have to do is call on the breath of God, and stay closely connected to the life of Jesus, the author of our faith. We don't have to program ourselves to death; we don't have to formulate our transition step-by-step; we don't have to count the uncountable. All we have to do is speak the new thing into being.

Jesus said,

"I assure you that I am the gate of the sheep. All who came before me were thieves and outlaws, but the sheep didn't listen to them. I am the gate. Whoever enters through me will be saved. They will come in and go out and find pasture. The thief enters only to steal, kill, and destroy. I came so that they could have life—indeed, so that they could live life to the fullest." (John 10:7-10)

Jesus is our only success. Jesus is our gate, our entrance to God's goodness. Others will say that we must attend to other things. But Jesus deserves our full attention. Follow him. Find life: life that is more beautiful than you've ever before imagined. For when the church rises again, her company will be great and will bring about world transformation, because love will reign and the kingdom of heaven will be on the earth.

All we have to do is restart.

Amen. May it be so.

NOTES

1. Looking for a ReStart

1. Rev. Billy Graham is quoted by Martin A. Davis Jr. in "Q&A: Leading Seminary Students Toward Renewal," *United Methodist Reporter*, October 15, 2008, accessed March 27, 2012, www.umportal.org/article.asp?id=4263.

2. This popular quote was not written by Wesley, but is often retold due to a conversation about preaching. See ThinkExist.com, "John Wesley Quotes," accessed March 29, 2012, http://thinkexist.com/quotes/john_wesley/.

3. John Wesley's quote: "My fear is not that our great movement, known as Methodists, will eventually cease to exist or one day die from the earth. My fear is that our people will become content to live without the fire, the power, the excitement, the supernatural element that makes us great." In Daily Christian Quote, "Christian Quotes by John Wesley Index," August 28, 2001, accessed March 29, 2012, http://dailychristianquote.com/dcqwesleyjohn.html.

4. *Association of Religion Data Archives*, "Evangelical Lutheran Church in America," accessed May 3, 2010, www.thearda.com/Denoms/D_1415.asp; and "United Methodist Church," www.thearda.com/Denoms/D_1469.asp.

5. Seth Godin, *The Dip: A Little Book That Teaches You When to Quit (And When to Stick)* (New York: Penguin, 2007), 17.

6. Ibid., 22.

7. Rebecca Barnes and Lindy Lowry, "Special Report: The American Church in Crisis," *Outreach*, May/June 2006, The Missional Church Network, http://missionalchurchnetwork.blogspot.com/2007/10/american-church-in-crisis.html.

8. Ibid.

9. Ibid.

10. Association of Religion Data Archives, "Evangelical Lutheran Church in America," accessed May 3, 2010, www.thearda.com/Denoms/D_1415.asp; and "United Methodist Church," www.thearda.com/Denoms/D_1469.asp.

11. *Online Etymology Dictionary*, accessed May 7, 2010, www.etymonline. com/index.php?search+re&searchmode=none.

12. Wayne Whitson Floyd, "Clergy Burnout," Alban Institute, August 23, 2010, accessed March 29, 2012, www.alban.org/conversation.aspx?id=9169.

13. Thomas G. Bandy, *Coaching Change: Breaking Down Resistance, Building Up Hope* (Nashville: Abingdon Press, 2000), 163–77.

14. Ibid., 172.

15. Colleen Shaddox, "The Real Flatliners," *Knowledge* 11 (June 2010): 62–67.

16. Ibid., 67.

17. Ibid., 62.

18. Joseph W. Daniels Jr., *Begging for Real Church* (Washington, D.C.: Beacon of Light Resources, 2009).

2. The Semiotics of Death

1. Peter Walsh, *Does This Clutter Make My Butt Look Fat?: An Easy Plan for Losing Weight and Living More* (New York: Free Press, 2008).

2. Andy Langford, ed., *The United Methodist Book of Worship* (Nashville: Abingdon Press, 1992).

3. John Flowers and Karen Vannoy, *10 Temptations of Church: Why Churches Decline and What to Do About It* (Nashville: Abingdon Press, 2012).

3. The Wild, Wild West

1. Adam Hamilton, "In 44 Years U.S. UMC to Be No More?" February 2009, accessed March 29, 2012, http://adamhamilton.cor.org/2009/02/12/in-44-years-us-umc-to-be-no-more/.

2. Lovett H. Weems Jr., *Focus: The Real Challenges That Face The United Methodist Church* (Nashville: Abingdon Press, 2011), 8.

3. *The Free Dictionary*, by Farlex, accessed February 15, 2012, http://www.thefreedictionary.com/cognition.

4. The Phrase Finder, "The Meaning and Origin of the Expression: Tit for Tat," accessed March 29, 2012, http://www.phrases.org.uk/meanings/tit-for-tat.html.

5. Seth Godin, *Tribes: We Need You to Lead Us* (New York: Penguin, 2008), 103–5.

4. Willing Heart, Not Leadership

1. Warren G. Bennis and Robert J. Thomas, *Geeks and Geezers: How Era, Values, and Defining Moments Shape Leaders* (Cambridge, Mass.: Harvard Business School, 2003). Quoted in Leonard Sweet, *Summoned to Lead* (Grand Rapids: Zondervan).

2. Sweet, *Summoned to Lead*, 33.

3. Ibid., 35–42.

4. Ibid., 77.

5. Jim Collins, *How the Mighty Fall: And Why Some Companies Never Give In* (New York: HarperCollins, 2009), 19–23.

6. In Collins, *How the Mighty Fall*, 120–22. Retold from William Manchester, *The Last Lion: Winston Spencer Churchill*, vol. 1, *Visions of Glory, 1874–1932* (New York: Little, Brown, 1983).

7. Collins, *How the Mighty Fall*, 122.

8. In Collins, *How the Mighty Fall*, 122–23. Story from the Churchill Centre, "Never Give In, Never, Never, Never," Selected Speeches of Winston Churchill, http://www.winstonchurchill.org/i4a/pages/index.cfm?pageid=423.

5. Fail Big and Fast; Get Up and Do It Again

1. Dictionary.com, http://dictionary.reference.com/browse/restore?s=t.

6. Be Creative

1. Leonard Sweet, *I Am a Follower: The Way, Truth, and Life of Following Jesus* (Nashville: Thomas Nelson, 2012), 43.

2. Sweet calls this "First Followers" in *I Am a Follower*. He states, "But first followers are always trying to get out of the way and make others first followers of Jesus as well" (27).

3. Ibid., 20.

4. John H. Wigger, *Taking Heaven by Storm: Methodism and the Rise of Popular Christianity in America* (Chicago: University of Illinois Press, 1998), 13.

5. Frank Baker, *A Charge to Keep: An Introduction to the People called Methodists* (London: Epworth Press, 1954), 18–19.

7. Fall in Love Again

1. Marianne Williamson, *A Return to Love: Reflections on the Principles of "A Course in Miracles"* (New York: HarperCollins, 1992), 190–91.

8. Go Deep with God

1. *Online Etymology Dictionary*, www.etymonline.com/index.php?term=release.

2. To see an updated list of the Wesley questions, see the webpage Grace Centered Forums, "John Wesley's Accountability Questions," June 27, 2006, accessed March 29, 2012, www.gracecentered.com/christian_forums/general-discussion/john-wesley's-accountability-questions/.

3. "Journal of John Wesley," in Christian Classics Ethereal Library, accessed March 29, 2012, www.ccel.org/ccel/wesley/journal.vi.ii.xvi.html.

4. Term used by Leonard Sweet in *I Am A Follower: The Way, Truth, and Life of Following Jesus* (Nashville: Thomas Nelson, 2012).

9. Stick with It

1. Eugene H. Peterson, *A Long Obedience in the Same Direction: Discipleship in an Instant Society* (Downers Grove, Ill.: InterVarsity Press, 2000), 16.

2. Ibid., 17.

3. Robert E. Webber, *Journey to Jesus: The Worship, Evangelism, and Nurture Mission of the Church* (Nashville: Abingdon Press, 2001), 11.

4. Mark Batterson, *Wild Goose Chase: Reclaim the Adventure of Pursuing God* (Colorado Springs: Multnomah, 2008), 35.

5. *Your Dictionary*, http://thesaurus.yourdictionary.com/reinvigorate.

6. Ibid.

7. Thomas A. Langford, *Wesleyan Theology: A Sourcebook* (Durham, N.C.: Labyrinth, 1984), 13–19.

8. Ibid.

10. Choose Jesus Over "Success"

1. Nadia Bolz-Weber, *Salvation on the Small Screen?: 24 Hours of Christian Television* (New York: Seabury, 2008).

2. Ibid., 17–18.

3. Ibid.